Andrew,

an excellen

Can't go b... ...

TRAVIS
G... 2:20
DEC 2020

# NOT ONE LITTLE CHILD:

## *A Biblical Critique of Calvinism*

Michael Cox
Senior Pastor
First Baptist Church
Pryor, Oklahoma

WESTBOW
P R E S S®
A DIVISION OF THOMAS NELSON
& ZONDERVAN

WestBow Press books may be ordered through booksellers or by contacting:

WestBow Press
A Division of Thomas Nelson & Zondervan
1663 Liberty Drive
Bloomington, IN 47403
www.westbowpress.com
1 (866) 928-1240

ISBN: 978-1-4908-9868-1 (sc)
ISBN: 978-1-4908-9867-4 (hc)

Library of Congress Control Number: 2016901758

Print information available on the last page.

WestBow Press rev. date: 02/05/2016

# BIOGRAPHICAL PROFILE OF THE WRITER

Michael A. Cox is a graduate of Southwestern Baptist Theological Seminary in Fort Worth, Texas, where he earned both Doctor of Ministry and Master of Divinity with Biblical Languages degrees, of Oklahoma State University in Stillwater, Oklahoma, where he earned a Bachelor of Arts degree in Religious Studies, and of New Orleans Baptist Theological Seminary in New Orleans, Louisiana, where he earned an Associate of Divinity degree in Pastoral Ministry. Licensed to preach in 1983 and ordained in 1984, he became Senior Pastor of First Baptist Church of Pryor, Oklahoma, in 2008. He came to Pryor, First, from West Lynchburg Baptist Church in Lynchburg, Virginia, where he served as Senior Pastor from 2003 until 2008. He went to West Lynchburg after serving as Pastor of Calvary Baptist Church in Inola, Oklahoma, from 1996-2003. He has also served as Pastor of the Lakeview Southern Baptist Church in Skiatook, Oklahoma, First Baptist Church of Boynton, Oklahoma, Oak Street Baptist Church in Cushing, Oklahoma, and Trinity Baptist Church in Keefeton, Oklahoma. In addition to his pastoral duties, he has also taught as an Adjunct Professor of Evangelism for Midwestern Baptist Theological Seminary's Tulsa extension.

# TABLE OF CONTENTS

# PREFACE

I have grown weary of searching for a book that would help me understand Calvinism and its attendant elements, like predestination, particularly a text which strikes a balance between being academic enough to be respected in the scholarly community, and yet practical enough to appeal to the wider audience comprised of the laity. Therefore, as with most of my writings, this present text is not intended to be too pedantic, but rather, is meant to be a blend between competent scholarship and practical information. However, balancing between the academic and the practical is not an easy task. If something is too academic (overly deep), few read it except for the pedants; and if it is too non-academic (overly shallow), few regard it as done competently enough to be worth reading. This study is very eclectic, bringing together, with comparative brevity, literally thousands of pages of material, as can be seen by my bibliography. Since one of my aims is to wed good scholarship with practical expression regarding layout, length, and overall readability, and do so utilizing an eclectic broadness, I truly believe that I have achieved my goal of producing a text which can help others better understand Calvinism and its accompanying elements. Striking this balance, then, has been an objective as I seek to examine Calvinism critically and scripturally.

My first textual aim is to provide a brief but informative historical and terminological survey of Calvinism and its concomitant elements. Next, my intent is to discuss Calvinism's strengths. Then the third and most significant purpose of this present work is to expound upon key biblical texts in an effort to hear what the Bible itself really has to say regarding Calvinism and its tenets. It is from this exposition of the Bible and from other related studies that twenty-five fatal weaknesses of Calvinism can be identified.

Lastly, I hold out little hope of converting Calvinists to my way of understanding the Bible on these matters. I am not naive enough to suppose that this present effort of mine will answer all the questions associated with Calvinism or put nails in Calvinism's coffin. Nevertheless, I operate with the conviction that ideas, like Calvinism, are fair game. Therefore, I hope to make a positive impact on all who read this work and especially pray that my effort will deter well-intending pilgrims from journeying down the ominous Calvinistic pathway.

Serving Christ,
Michael A. Cox
Pryor, Oklahoma
July 2009

# CHAPTER 1: PREDESTINATION

## Definitions

Definitions of predestination abound. Some explanations of the word stress the creedal, or doctrinal, nuance, such as that of Ron Glass, former Associate Professor of Bible Exposition, Talbot School of Theology, La Mirada, California, when he writes that predestination is "the doctrine that God has planned everything that comes to pass."[1] But does such a definition not plainly make God the author of sin? Likewise, the deterministic connotation is even more evident and the absolute authorship of God in all things, including sin, is clearly pronounced in the definition of the late Calvinistic author Loraine Boettner when he writes, "From eternity God has predetermined or foreordained all things which come to pass, including the final salvation or reprobation of all human beings."[2] Similarly, popular Calvinistic commentator Matthew Henry states that even the death of each individual has already been appointed by God,[3] presumably

---

[1] Ron Glass, "Election in the Old Testament," in *The Holman Bible Handbook*, ed. David S. Dockery (Nashville, TN: Holman Bible Publishers, 1992), 402.

[2] Loraine Boettner, "Predestination," in *Baker's Dictionary of Theology*, ed. Everett F. Harrison, Geoffrey W. Bromiley, and Carl F. H. Henry (Grand Rapids, MI: Baker Book House, 1960), 415.

[3] Matthew Henry, *An Exposition with Practical Observations of the Gospel According to St. John* in *Matthew Henry's Commentary on the Whole Bible*, vol. 5, *Matthew to John* (McLean, VA: McDonald Publishing Company, n.d.; reprint, n.d.), 1233.

implying that even mishaps and murders have been blueprinted by the Almighty.

I contend that these definitions are more than simply inadequate. They are evangelically alarming and distasteful at best and evangelically negligent and blasphemous at worst. In fact, Henry's words, leaving no room for mishaps or accidents, conflict greatly with teachings from the Book of Proverbs which intimate the shortening of life due to ungodly living (Prov. 9:11). In order to be consistent, Henry would have had to say that God appointed the loose living which caused the death just as God appointed the death itself. Henry further argues that, just as it is appointed to each person to die once (Heb. 9:27), the kind of death is also appointed by God.[4] This is classic eisegesis and pressing far more meaning into the word "appointed" than Scripture intends.

Most people in general, and Christians in particular, would agree that the aforementioned definitions of predestination can be greatly improved. The word predestination comes from the Greek (the language of the New Testament documents) word *proorizo*, which W. E. Vine says is to be distinguished from foreknowing, and has special reference to that to which the subjects of God's foreknowledge are predestinated.[5] Arndt and Gingrich say that predestination is to decide upon beforehand,[6] which proffers a cautious definition, like that of Vine, being thoughtfully careful not to saddle God with the authorship of evil. While God is ultimately responsible for the *fact* of human freedom, He is not immediately responsible for the *acts* of human freedom.[7]

---

[4]  Ibid.

[5]  W. E. Vine, *Vine's Expository Dictionary of New Testament Words* (McLean, VA: MacDonald Publishing Company, n.d.), 885.

[6]  William F. Arndt, and F. Wilbur Gingrich, *A Greek-English Lexicon of the New Testament and Other Early Christian Literature*, 2d ed. (Chicago, IL: The University of Chicago Press, 1979), 709.

[7]  See Norman L. Geisler, *Christian Apologetics* (Grand Rapids, MI: Baker Book House, 1976; reprint 2002), 231.

## Fullest Expression

Boettner says that the fullest expression of predestination is found in the Westminster Confession of Faith, which is the authoritative standard for most Presbyterian and Reformed churches, and that typical Reformed confessions are infralapsarian,[8] which will be discussed later. Regarding the history of predestination, Boettner further explains that the doctrine was left largely undeveloped by patristic writers for the first three Christian centuries.[9] Such a chronologically lengthy period of omission immediately raises questions as to why those closest to the Apostles did not expound upon such a seemingly significant concept.

## History

Gregg Singer, former Chairman of the Department of History at Catawba College, Salisbury, North Carolina, says that predestination apparently received its first full exposition by Augustine (354-430) as a result of his debate with Pelagius (354-418).[10] It is worth noting that the full development of Augustine's doctrine of predestination did not occur until the last decade of his life and was propelled largely by the stress of the Pelagian controversy.[11]

Augustine taught that Lucifer and all the other angels were created good, but that they exercised their freewills and chose to sin. Alister McGrath, Professor of Historical Theology, Oxford University, Oxford, England, says that Augustine further taught that before the Fall of Adam and Eve mankind was innocent, immortal, and possessed a freewill, but after the Fall spiritual death occurred and physical death entered the world of man.[12] Augustine proposed that in Adam and Eve

---

[8]   Boettner, "Predestination," 415-6.

[9]   Ibid., 415.

[10]  Gregg C. Singer, "Augustinianism," in *Baker's Dictionary of Theology*, ed. Everett F. Harrison, Geoffrey W. Bromiley, and Carl F. H. Henry (Grand Rapids, MI: Baker Book House, 1960), 80.

[11]  Saint Augustine, *Confessions*, trans. Henry Chadwick (New York, NY: Oxford University Press, 1991; reprint, 1998). See Chadwick's footnote 29 on page 293.

[12]  Alister E. McGrath, *Justification by Faith: What It Means to Us Today* (Grand Rapids, MI: Academie Books, 1988), 39.

the entire human race fell from its previous glory and, through Adam, sin was passed from *father* to child, from generation to generation.[13] He said that "the feebleness of infant limbs is innocent, not the infant's mind."[14] Notice the Augustinian emphasis of the sin nature being passed from father to child and the omission of any sin nature being passed from mother to child. This appears to be preparatory for the later assertion by many Calvinists that Jesus possessed no sin nature, since he had no earthly father. Such a doctrine, however, makes Jesus less than human, is not drawn from Scripture, and virtually discards the fully human characteristics and nature carried by mothers, who are, by the way, fully human themselves. This I will explore in a later section. Meanwhile, more from Augustine. He believed that mankind's nature is now corrupt, at least those with an earthly father, that man's will is enslaved to sin, and that man's choice can be exercised relative only to civil laws. In other words, Augustine maintained that mankind's will to choose good was not merely damaged, but completely destroyed by the Fall, although he seemed at times to indicate that his "mutable nature deviated by its own choice and that error is its punishment."[15] He admitted that he had been taught that free choice of the will was the reason why people do wrong and suffer just judgment, but confessed that he could never get a clear grasp of this.[16] Keep this Augustinian definition of "totally depraved" in mind, for it differs radically from the dominant, and orthodox, evangelical position. He further asserted that sin is present at conception and that a special work of God's Word and Spirit are necessary to believe, repent, and continue to believe. The late Robert Baker, longtime Professor of Church History at Southwestern Baptist Theological Seminary in Fort Worth, Texas, explains that Augustine also taught that grace is irresistible for the elect, and that baptism, including infant baptism, is necessary for salvation because the

---

[13]  Ibid., 40.
[14]  Augustine, 1.10, 9.
[15]  Ibid., 4.26, 68.
[16]  Ibid., 7.5, 113-4.

guilt of original sin is inherited and must be washed away.[17] Augustine continued to echo his mother's belief that being washed in the "saving water of baptism" was necessary, and sacramental, following infant baptism.[18] Clearly, he embraced the doctrine of baptismal regeneration[19] and the miraculous nature of the Eucharist as a sacrament "to initiate and convert 'uninstructed and unbelieving people.'"[20] In order to facilitate the salvation process, said Augustine, God provides special graces. The first is called *prevenient* grace, which is grace shown by God prior to man's response,[21] the second is dubbed *cooperative* grace, which is the grace said to be in tact until glorification, and the third and final grace installment Augustine calls *effective* grace, which he said takes over for resurrection purposes. Further, double-predestination is the Augustinian teaching that particular individuals are chosen to be saved while others are destined for damnation because God chose not to intervene in their lives and elect them for salvation. But, strangely, Augustine, in seeming contradiction to other deterministic doctrines, asserted that God does not desert anything He has made![22]

I recognize a brilliant thinker in Augustine, but I do not regard him as a sound interpreter of the Bible or as a well-grounded theologian. One of the primary problems with Augustine's theology is the grid through which he interpreted Scripture. His hermeneutical (interpretive) method was frightfully faulty from the start because he unwisely employed the Neoplatonism of his day in developing his theology.[23] The late John Newport, Distinguished Professor of Philosophy of Religion, Emeritus, at Southwestern Baptist Theological Seminary in Fort Worth, Texas, tells us that Neoplatonism (a "newer"

---

[17] Robert A. Baker, *A Summary of Christian History* (Nashville, TN: Broadman Press, 1959), 79.

[18] Augustine, 6.23, 107.

[19] Ibid., 9.3, 158.

[20] Ibid., 13.27, 299.

[21] McGrath, *Justification by Faith*, 133.

[22] Augustine, 5.1, 72.

[23] Singer, 80. His use of Neoplatonism and Plotinus is evident throughout his *Confessions*.

or revived version of the doctrines of the ancient Greek philosopher Plato which blossoms from the rational of Platonism to the mystical of Neoplatonism) teaches that there is only one true reality, the spiritual reality, and that the real world is the unseen world of Ideas or Forms, upon which the physical - material universe is patterned.[24] Notice Neoplatonism's emphasis upon the reality of the metaphysical, meaning the abstract, intangible, and unseen, and the denigrating of the physical, meaning the substantive, tangible, and seen. Thus, a hermeneutic (method of interpretation) based on Neoplatonism is going to read Scripture with the definite intention of "discovering" the abstract, intangible, and unseen i.e., the hidden things. Augustine and plenty of others after him are woefully allegorical in their exegesis of Scripture, routinely "discovering" unsubstantiated hidden meanings that careful interpreters will recognize as eisegesis, which means reading into the text something that is not present, whereas exegesis is simply letting the text speak for itself by drawing out the facts. Even the popular Calvinist exegete Matthew Henry, while taking the Bible literally, customarily ascertains allegorical meanings and applications in Scripture. Additionally, Neoplatonism teaches that there exists a hierarchy of Ideas (Forms, Realities), with the ultimate Idea sitting atop the heap being hailed as the One, from which the subordinate Nous (the Mind or the light of Intellect) emanated, from the likes of which the further inferior World Soul sprang.[25] Neoplatonism argues that individual human souls come from the World Soul, and the manyness of the material world comes from something lower in rank below the World Soul.[26] Further, Augustine's Neoplatonism claims that the religious task is to reclaim oneself from the One by retracing the path of downward emanation from the One by an upward ascent of the soul.[27] Hinduism, Buddhism, and the New Age movement, all of

---

[24] John P. Newport, *The New Age Movement and the Biblical Worldview: Conflict and Dialogue* (Grand Rapids, MI: William B. Eerdmans Publishing Co., 1998), 20.
[25] Ibid., 20-1.
[26] Ibid., 21.
[27] Ibid.

which teach reincarnation, are very comfortable with Neoplatonism's upward ascent theory, but attentive evangelical believers in Jesus Christ will find no place for such gnostic hypotheses in biblical Christianity. Still further, Neoplatonism seeks mystical experience, which it calls union with the One.[28] It also freely employs dualism, which is the philosophy that two *equally powerful* forces, one good and one evil, are at work in the universe. Dualism, however, is not the orthodox Christian view. While it is true that biblical Christianity teaches that there are two opposing forces, the biblical triune God and Satan, orthodox Christianity vehemently denies that Satan is anywhere near as powerful as the biblical triune God.

How much Neoplatonism crept into Augustine's exegetical work? I do not know, but it was too much for me to be comfortable with any of his hermeneutical conclusions, because looking at Scripture through his neoplatonic grid undoubtedly led to gross interpretive distortion, since such an interpretive methodology is eisegetical by nature, forcing conformity to the flawed neoplatonic system rather than allowing the texts themselves to speak plainly by employing a grammatical-historical interpretive methodology, which is far and away more precise and faithful to the contexts of Scripture. As I stated above, Augustine was committed to the allegorical interpretation of the Bible, placing a premium on the unusual and surprising "hidden meanings," "figurative interpretations,"[29] or "secret meaning"[30] allegedly waiting to be discovered, an approach he admired in Ambrose, former Bishop of Milan.[31] In my estimation, everything Augustine said is suspect. He may be brilliantly biblical in one doctrine (the freewills of man and angels before the Fall), and yet inexplicably unbiblical (infant baptism to wash away the guilt of original sin)[32] in another. Augustine is not the fellow I am trusting for help in understanding the doctrine of

---

28 Ibid.
29 Augustine, 5.24, 88.
30 Ibid., 6.8, 96.
31 John P. Newport, *What Is Christian Doctrine?* (Nashville, TN: Broadman Press, 1984), 45.
32 Augustine, 5.15, 81.

predestination and its cousins because his hermeneutical method was, although probably very sincere, troublingly atrocious.

Unfortunately, Anselm (1033-1109), Peter Lombard (1095-1160), and the iridescent and indubitably influential Catholic theologian Thomas Aquinas (1224-1274) followed Augustine, identifying predestination as God's providential control over all things. Aquinas taught that the (Catholic) Church is the bridge between God and man, and that Christ channeled the (seven) sacraments by way of the Church, thus enabling man to do good works after baptism. Aquinas further taught that the grace of God is attained through baptism, then, subsequently, the other sacraments provide vehicles of enablement to do good works and merit salvation. For Aquinas, then, salvation consisted of grace and works together, with grace being infused at baptism and the work of the sacraments following automatically. Like Aquinas who followed Augustine, John Wycliffe (1330-1384) and John Huss (1372-1415) also held to his ideas on predestination, as did the more familiar names of Martin Luther (1483-1546), Philip Melanchthon (1497-1560), and John Calvin (1509-1564), all of whom were steeped in Augustinianism and Aquinan Catholicism, although they would begin to gravitate away from the latter as they commenced to do the unthinkable -- read the Bible for themselves, study the original languages, and attempt to interpret the contents of Scripture forthrightly.

Martin Luther (1483-1546)[33] was an Augustinian monk[34] who became rather disenchanted with a number of Catholic practices, but exploring Luther's contentions with the Catholic church are beyond the scope of my present effort. He was certainly one of the sharpest knives in the drawer. Nevertheless, while it is true that Luther discarded some unwanted, and clearly unscriptural, Catholic practices and doctrines,

---

[33] Otto Weber, *Foundations of Dogmatics*, vol.1, trans. Darrell L. Guder (Neukirchen, Germany: Kreis Moers, 1955; reprint, Grand Rapids, MI: William B. Eerdmans Publishing Co., 1988), 104.

[34] George Johnson, Jerome D. Hannan, and Sister M. Dominica, *The Story of the Church: Her Founding, Mission and Progress* (New York, NY: Benzinger Brothers, Inc., 1946), 302.

he held tenaciously to his Augustinianism regarding the late Bishop of Hippo's ideas on predestination, election, the work of the "graces," and the human will. In 1525 Luther wrote *Bondage of the Will*,[35] in which he argued that there are two wills of God: the *hidden* and the *revealed*.[36] For Luther, the hidden will of God was unwritten and found only in God Himself. In other words it was not recorded as Scripture. To him, this meant that only certain individuals would be enabled to respond to God's inward call, whereas the revealed will of God, which is God's written word, commands one to respond to Scripture. But Luther's distinction in the wills of God establishes an authority higher than the written word of God, none other than God Himself; yet, while the written word of God can be verified objectively, one cannot verify God Himself apart from the written word, which creates a terribly subjective mode for knowing God removed from His word.

Luther also argued that the highest degree of faith is to believe that God is merciful, although "He saves so few and damns so many."[37] He was convinced that people were captive either to God's will or to Satan's will and that man's will was "like a beast standing between two riders" which went wherever the rider willed.[38] And no man can choose his rider or even seek his rider, for the riders themselves fight to decide who will ride.[39] So, Luther's treatise denied the possibility of free choice for humans concerning salvation and argued that man's will, even in other matters, is overruled by the freewill of God because man is but a captive either to the will of God or to the will of Satan,[40] although he conceded that man's freewill can do some things by nature like eat, drink, beget, rule, and so forth.[41] He contended that if God does not

---

[35] Weber, 55.

[36] Martin Luther, *The Bondage of the Will* (trans. J. I. Packer and O. R. Johnston), 4.10 (N.p.: James Clarke & Co. Ltd., 1957; reprint, Grand Rapids, MI: Fleming H. Revell, 2004), 169.

[37] Ibid., 2.7, 101.

[38] Ibid., 2.8, 103.

[39] Ibid., 2.8, 104.

40 Ibid., 2.9, 107.

[41] Ibid., 5.7, 265.

act on a man's behalf, that man is doomed. But, while there is obviously truth in the statement that man is doomed without God acting on his behalf by sending Christ and by initiating contact with man in salvation, it is Luther's explanation of this statement that misses the mark, for he said that God produces the faith in the heart of the person [if the person is one of the elect], which is passive not active, in that it is produced independently of the person.[42] I intend to deal with this in more detail in a later section, but I can tell you that this tenet seems to make no distinction between the active and passive voices inherent in Greek grammar and heeded by those following the grammatical-historical method of biblical hermeneutics.

Philip Melanchthon (1497-1560) initially followed Martin Luther's views on predestination and election. Later, however, he modified his convictions, upsetting some Lutherans by teaching freedom of the will in salvation.[43] For a man of such a time and training, this assertion was a radical departure from tenaciously held Augustinian dictums.

This brief historical survey now brings us to the man himself, John Calvin (1509-1564). Calvin set forth and promoted the Augustinian dogma of predestination so clearly and emphatically that the doctrines associated with predestinarianism were dubbed "Calvinism" by the German Lutheran polemicist Joachim Westphal (1510-1574) as a reference to the theological and sacramental views of the Swiss Reformers in general and to John Calvin in particular.[44] He prodigiously increased the usage of Augustine by citing the Bishop of Hippo's doctrines in his voluminous writings, *Institutes of the Christian Religion*. Like Augustine, Calvin eventually advanced to "double-predestination," which asserts that there are two classes of people: the elect and the non-elect.[45] He declared that the non-elect are reprobates who are passed over and not

---

[42]  Ibid., 4.16, 187. See also 7.16, 311.

[43]  Weber, 107.

[44]  Alister E. McGrath, *Evangelicalism & the Future of Christianity* (Downers Grove, IL: InterVarsity Press, 1995), 54.

[45]  John Calvin, *Institutes of the Christian Religion*, 4th ed. trans. Henry Beveridge (N.p.: 1581; reprint; *The New American Standard Electronic Bible Library*, La Habra, CA: The Lockman Foundation, 1999), 3.21.5.

given saving grace by God.[46] He said that God hardens their hearts and cited Rom. 9:17 as evidence for this. He went on to claim that some are prepared for destruction and drew upon Rom. 9:22 for biblical support, arguing that they are appointed to doom, citing 1 Pet. 2:8, and are marked out for destruction beforehand, referencing Jude 4.

In hindsight, one might opine that the Reformers probably over-reacted to Catholicism's emphasis upon the works of man for salvation by polarizing the other direction, making salvation the absolute work of God with virtually no involvement from man, not even repentance and faith. To be sure, Catholicism's emphasis on the works of man needed to be exposed as unbiblical, but Calvin's views are as out of balance the opposite direction. After the death of Calvin, sometimes called the "Protestant Pope," Calvinism was systematized and simplified by William Perkins as a result of his debate with Jacob Arminius.

Jacob Arminius (1560-1609) disagreed with Calvin on several points. He taught that mankind's will was indeed wounded but not rendered inoperative by the Fall of Adam. Like Calvin, he believed that the Holy Spirit could enable man to respond to the gospel, but, unlike Calvin, Arminius asserted that mankind's response to the gospel is conditionally, not unconditionally, predetermined. He further taught that mankind can choose to accept or reject God's overtures, and this includes the elect. He said that the death of Christ was on behalf of all of humanity, thus, the atonement was unlimited in its scope, which is known as belief in a *general* view of the atonement as opposed to a *particular*, or *limited*, view of it.[47] Opposite Calvin and Perkins, Arminius said that the grace, or unmerited favor, of God can be resisted and that a believer can become an unbeliever, since some may not persevere. The views of Arminius were forcefully declared in 1610, one year after his death, by his followers in the Netherlands, who published a five article document, called a remonstrance, which is

---

[46] J. I. Packer, "Predestination," in *The New Bible Dictionary*, ed. J. D. Douglas (Grand Rapids, MI: William B. Eerdmans Publishing Co., 1962), 1026.

[47] Justo L. Gonzales, *The Story of Christianity: The Reformation to the Present Day*, vol. 2 (San Francisco, CA: Harper & Row, Publishers, 1985), 181.

a protest, challenging five aspects of Calvinism. It is now customary to label followers of Arminius as "Remonstrants."[48]

William Perkins (1558-1602) is the man primarily responsible for systematizing Calvinism.[49] He purposely defined strict Calvinism in response to the five propositions opined by Jacob Arminius and his followers. The retort of Perkins is known as "Five Point Calvinism," or the "TULIP Theory," since TULIP serves as the acrostic designed to simplify and aid remembrance of the five points of Calvinism.[50]

The first point argues that mankind's will was not only wounded, but also became **T**otally depraved (human impotence) as a result of the Fall; yet, the Holy Spirit can enable man to respond to the gospel. On his own, however, mankind is so totally depraved that he cannot even respond affirmatively to God.

The second point contends that mankind's response to the gospel is absolutely **U**nconditional; thus the elect were selected by God with no input regarding the decision and with no consideration by God of future conduct. The same holds true for the non-elect. God's election and non-election are completely absolute, unqualified, and inappealable.

The third point asserts that the death of Christ was on behalf of the elect and only the elect; thus, the atonement is **L**imited, also called particular, only to them.

The fourth point declares that the grace, or unmerited favor, of God is **I**rresistible. The elect will inevitably believe and doing so is utterly unpreventable.

And, the fifth, and final, point of Calvinism maintains that a believer cannot become an unbeliever, thus claiming that all of the elect will **P**ersevere. Unconditional election insures the irresistibility of grace and the continuance of faith.

---

[48] Fisher Humphreys, and Paul E. Robertson. *God So Loved the World: Traditional Baptists and Calvinism* (New Orleans, LA: Insight Press, 2000), 13.

[49] Weber, 124.

[50] Frank S. Mead, *Handbook of Denominations in the United States*, 8th ed., rev. Samuel S. Hill (Nashville, TN: Abingdon Press, 1985), 206.

## Related Scriptures on Predestination

Calvinists use the Bible to support their views.[51] Calvinism teaches that God ordains one's substance and days (Ps. 139:16), asserts that Christ's work of redemption was known all along by God and predetermined (Acts 2:23; 4:27-28), and argues that some are appointed to eternal life (Acts 13:48). It also contends that God foreknows (Rom. 8:29), predestines (Rom. 8:29), calls (Rom. 8:30), justifies (Rom. 8:30), glorifies (Rom. 8:30), chooses (Rom. 9:11-12), prepares beforehand (Rom. 9:23), predestines wisdom for man's glory (1 Cor. 2:7), and foreordains some to adoption (Eph. 1:5). Calvinism further declares that God decided beforehand that believers should walk in good works (Eph. 2:10), and God predestines the obtaining of an inheritance for all believers (Eph. 2:11). Nevertheless, citing these Scriptures is a far cry from supporting Total Depravity, as Calvinists understand it, or substantiating Unconditional Election, Limited Atonement, and Irresistible Grace. To say that God elects some is not the same thing as saying that God bypasses others, leaving them no hope of ever being redeemed. Therefore, an exploration of election is in order and it is to this that we now turn.

---

[51] Boettner, "Predestination," 416.

# CHAPTER 2: ELECTION

## Views on the Fall of Man

A discussion of election might best be prefaced by explaining the primary schools of thought opining when election occurs. There are two principal views regarding the Fall of man: the *supralapsarian* and the *infralapsarian*.

The supralapsarian view argues that election *preceded* the Fall. Supralapsarian proponents posit the following chronology, saying that (1) God proposed to elect some individuals to salvation and condemn others to destruction, (2) God then proposed to create, (3) God proposed to permit the Fall, (4) God proposed to send Christ to redeem only the elect, and, (5) God proposed to send the Holy Spirit to apply redemption only to the elect.[52]

On the other hand, the infralapsarian view contends that election *followed* the Fall. Infralapsarian proponents posit the following chronology, saying that (1) God proposed to create, (2) God proposed to permit the Fall, (3) God proposed to elect some out of this fallen mass to be saved and leave others as they were, (4) God proposed to provide a Redeemer only for the elect, and, (5) God proposed to send the Holy Spirit to apply redemption only to the elect.[53]

---

[52] Ibid., 417.
[53] Ibid.

# Definitions

Definitions of election offered by theologians abound. Boettner says that the word election is found approximately forty-eight times in the New Testament. He writes, "It sets forth an eternal, divine decree which, antecedently to any difference or desert in men themselves, separates the human race into two portions, one of which is chosen to everlasting life, while the other is left to everlasting death."[54] Boettner further states,

> A portion of the race, the elect members, are rescued from the state of guilt and sin, and are brought into a state of blessedness and holiness. The non-elect are simply left in their previous state of ruin.[55]

Kurt Richardson, former Assistant Professor of Historical Theology at Southeastern Baptist Theological Seminary in Wake Forest, North Carolina, says election is "an action of God prior to and independent of any human action or condition."[56] The same writer further declares that election is "that will and action of God to call undeserving persons to share in his glory."[57] The Greek adjective *eklektos* means picked out, chosen, or elected.[58] The Bible teaches that Christ Himself was the *chosen* one of God to be the Messiah (Luke 23:35). Angels are said to be *chosen* to be of high ranking administrative association with God (1 Tim. 5:21). Believers were *chosen* (Matt. 24:22, 24, 31; Mark 13:20, 22, 27; Luke 18:7; Rom. 8:33; Col. 3:12; 2 Tim. 2:10) in Christ before the foundation of the world (Eph. 1:4), *chosen* to adoption (Eph. 1:5), *chosen* to good works (Eph. 2:10), and *chosen* to conformity to Christ (Rom. 8:29). Also, the human will has nothing to do with *God's* election (Eph. 1:4, 5; Rom. 9:11; 11:5). Further, believers are given by God the

---

[54] Ibid.

[55] Ibid.

[56] Kurt A. Richardson, "Election in the New Testament," in *The Holman Bible Handbook*, ed. David S. Dockery (Nashville, TN: Holman Bible Publishers, 1992), 712.

[57] Ibid.

[58] Vine, 361-2.

Father to Christ as the fruit of His death, and are all foreknown and foreseen by God (John 17:6; Rom. 8:29). Vine contends that, "while Christ's death was sufficient for all men, and is effective in the case of the elect, yet men are treated as responsible, being capable of the will and power to choose."[59] Notice here that Vine defends the concept of the freewill of man. Arndt and Gingrich simply define the elect as those whom God has chosen from the generality of mankind and drawn to Himself.[60]

The noun *ekloge* means selection, or that which is chosen.[61] Its usages include God's choice of Saul of Tarsus (Acts 9:15), of Jacob (Rom. 9:11), and of the remnant, i.e., believing Jews (Rom. 11:5). It may mean the act of choosing or it may designate the ones chosen, and frequently implies the chosen instrument used, and is especially indicative of God's selection of Christians (2 Pet. 1:10).[62]

## Election in the Old Testament

Ron Glass says that election has particular reference to God's decision "prior to creation" (notice that Glass adopts the supralapsarian, i.e., prior to creation, view). Glass states that the Old Testament uses the term elect in relation to three subjects: (1) the nation of Israel, (2) a select group of prominent leaders in Israel to preserve her as the covenant community, and (3) the elect servant.[63]

The first of these three references to election in the Old Testament asserts that the choice of the nation of Israel was an election to be God's covenant community (Isa. 45:4), to reveal His sovereignty and holiness to the nations, to be the vehicle for bringing forth the Messiah, and to be His inheritance (Deut. 7:6; 10:5).[64] But, as J. I. Packer, Board of Governors Professor of Theology, Regent College, Vancouver, British Columbia, rightly asserts, religious and ethical obligations are created

---

[59] Ibid.
[60] Arndt, 242.
[61] Vine, 362.
[62] Arndt, 243.
[63] Glass, 402.
[64] Richardson, 712.

by election.[65] Packer also correctly, in my estimation, points out that the promised blessings of election for Israel were forfeited through unbelief and disobedience.[66] One can only surmise, then, that the elect had a choice, which is precisely where Packer and I are likely to part company. Refusal to accept God's invitation, elect or non-elect, means one is not the Lord's, and these will be dealt with accordingly (Jer. 5:10). Moreover, Old Testament election was to service; hence, salvation was not automatic, regardless of one's status as "elect": the lostness of the Pharisees is an ample case in point (John 8:44). Packer helps us see that the national election of Israel implies the presence of a stricter judgment upon national sin (Amos 3:2).[67] But, Packer believes that there is an election to *privilege* and an election to *life*.[68] He says that the *entire nation* of Israel was elected to the privilege of living under the covenant, and that those *made faithful by regeneration* are the ones whom God had chosen out of the nation of Israel for election to life.[69] Notice carefully that Packer, like other Calvinists, argues for regeneration as that which is done *prior to* the faith event. This is known as the doctrine of monergistic regeneration, which states that the faith which receives Christ Jesus for justification is a free gift of the sovereign God and is, itself, bestowed *by regeneration* in the act of effectual calling.[70] So Packer, like Luther before him, clearly supposes that regeneration *precedes* faith and, in fact, makes faith possible. Calvinist Thomas Nettles, Professor of Historical Theology at The Southern Baptist Theological Seminary in Louisville, Kentucky, echoes the same doctrine when he writes an exposition of Article 5a of *The Baptist Faith and Message* saying, "Regeneration by the Spirit of God shatters the shackles of sin and its tyrannical power by creating such

---

[65] J. I. Packer, "Election," in *The New Bible Dictionary*, ed. J. D. Douglas (Grand Rapids, MI: William B. Eerdmans Publishing Co., 1962), 358.

[66] Ibid., 359.

[67] Ibid., 358.

[68] Ibid., 359.

[69] Ibid.

[70] Packer and Johnston in their "Historical and Theological Introduction" to Luther's *The Bondage of the Will*, 58.

distaste for sin that the sinner repents."[71] So, for Nettles, regeneration *precedes* repentance, a position which flies directly into the face of the ministry of John the Baptist, who baptized the repentant in preparation for the arrival of the Messiah, in whom the penitent would believe upon His unveiling (Matt. 3:1-12). As for Packer's references to election to privilege and to life, is this a "double-election," whereby the entire nation of Israel was elected to service, then certain ones of the nation were elected to salvation? Packer seems to think so, and believes that the rest forfeited their opportunity to inherit the riches of the relationship to God which the covenant held out because of their unbelief.[72] Obviously, Packer recognizes the problem of some of the "elect" of Israel disobeying and resisting God. John the Baptist clearly explained that being related to Abraham was insufficient for being exempted from God's eternal wrath of fire (Matt. 3:9-10). Packer attempts to address the problem of the renegade "elect" by essentially admitting that not all of the chosen of Israel inherited eternal life. He does this by conveniently creating another category for election, that of *privilege*. However, this arbitrary innovation begs the question as to whether or not all those elected to privilege inherited the favors and blessings. Even a cursory reading of the Old Testament would produce a resounding "no!" to this question. Thus, when Packer argues that many of those elected to privilege forfeited their opportunity to inherit the riches of the relationship to God because of their unbelief, the same must be said of those elected to life (salvation). He recognizes that not all those elected to privilege inherited the blessings. In other words, election to privilege could be forfeited according to Packer. Since election to privilege could be forfeited, election in itself does not automatically produce positive results. Therefore, since election to privilege does not produce automatic results, what about election to eternal life? Would Packer agree that it, too, can be forfeited? Hardly. Nevertheless, his attempted resolution implodes upon itself because he

---

[71] Thomas J. Nettles, "Article 5a: God's Purpose of Grace and Election," *The Baptist Banner*, May 2004, 4.

[72] Packer, "Election," 359.

stubbornly refuses to acknowledge the factor of the human will, which I will discuss in a later section.

The second of these three references to election in the Old Testament teaches that a select group of prominent leaders in Israel was chosen to preserve Israel as the covenant community. This can be seen in God's choice of Moses as Israel's prototypical intercessor (Ps. 106:23), and God's selection of David as the recipient of the kingly (Davidic) covenant (Ps. 89:3).

The third, and last, of these three references to election in the Old Testament is that of the appointment of the elect servant (Isa. 42:1-4), Israel's Messiah, whom Christians know to be the Lord Jesus Christ. Scripture asserts that His reign and His work of redemption were indisputably preordained from eternity (Acts 2:23; 1 Pet. 1:20).

## Election in the New Testament

Kurt Richardson explains, rightly I surmise, that election in the New Testament means that believers have become the elect through their personal faith in Christ.[73] Richardson does not appear to place regeneration chronologically ahead of personal faith. On the other hand, John Murray, former Professor of Systematic Theology at Westminster Theological Seminary in Philadelphia, Pennsylvania, like most Calvinists, argues, perhaps circularly, that salvation in possession is proof of election.[74] I have always found it amusing that those writing and speaking of election, are, of course, the elect, are they not? But how can they know? This is one of the contentions of Christian author and apologist Dave Hunt throughout his book, *What Love Is This?: Calvinism's Misrepresentation of God*. Hunt points out repeatedly the ambiguity of the statement that "salvation in possession is proof of election," stressing all the while the fact that Calvinism offers no firm

---

[73] Richardson, 712.

[74] John Murray, "Elect, Election," in *Baker's Dictionary of Theology*, ed. Everett F. Harrison, Geoffrey W. Bromiley, and Carl F. H. Henry (Grand Rapids, MI: Baker Book House, 1960), 180.

way of *knowing* that one is saved. One wonders, mystifyingly, how the clarity of John 3:16 and Rom. 10:9-10 can be missed.

I contend that Apostles, like Peter, Paul, and James, had difficulty believing that God would choose to include Gentiles in His redemptive activity and that some prophets, like Jonah, angrily resented such a soteriology (doctrine of salvation) and disobediently resisted participation in bringing it to fruition. Their elective exclusivity had to be overcome, their theological misunderstandings had to be corrected, and their racial prejudices had to be obliterated. As I will discuss in more detail later, it took a vision from God for Peter to have his exclusively Jewish frame of elective reference thoroughly shattered for him to recognize that all humans are created in God's image and are, therefore, targets of His redemptive activity (Acts 10:9-16). Jonah's lesson concerning God's compassion for all people was not as pleasant.

The late Herschel Hobbs, longtime Southern Baptist pastor, writer, and denominational activist, in his commentary on *The Baptist Faith and Message* reminds that the freewill of man and his power of choice must not be overlooked when exploring election.[75] He argues that election should not be regarded as God's purpose to save as *few* as possible, but that the tenor of the Bible echoes the fact that God loves all and wishes to save as *many* as possible.[76] Hobbs maintains that election should never be viewed as the saving of some and the neglect of others, arguing that if some are saved and others are lost regardless of what they do or do not do, what incentive is there to seek the Lord and preach the gospel?[77] Like the vast majority of evangelicals, Hobbs asserts that man is not a puppet on a string and argues that election never appears in the Bible as mechanical or as blind destiny, eloquently stating that to "draw" is God's initiative and to "come" is man's response.[78] I believe that the word "call" necessarily implies "answer."

---

[75]  Herschel H. Hobbs, *The Baptist Faith and Message* (Nashville, TN: Convention Press, 1981), 65.
[76]  Ibid.
[77]  Ibid.
[78]  Ibid.

Like the divine and human natures of Christ being paradoxically combined without confusion, God's sovereignty and man's freewill must both be recognized in salvation and in life. In other words, the incarnation of Jesus Christ provides a sound hermeneutical paradigm for accurately handling and correctly understanding a number of theological mysteries, namely Christology (the doctrine of the nature of Christ) and soteriology.

The incarnation of Jesus Christ is the criterion by which all Scripture should be interpreted. Orthodox theology recognizes the presence of both the human and the divine natures in Him. To deny the obvious presence of both is heresy. Likewise, the Bible itself is manifestly a product of both the human and the divine elements, being 100 percent inspired by God and 100 percent penned by men who used their own vocabularies. The writing of the Bible, then, was unmistakably both a human and a divine enterprise. Further, I am aggressively affirming that salvation involves both the grace and sovereignty of God and the faith, repentance, and freewill of man; and when I say freewill, I mean unlimited freewill, opposite Calvinists, who use the word freewill, but do not mean the same thing. After listening to R. C. Sproul at one of his conferences in Houston, Texas, in 1998, I know that, for him, freewill means that one can make any decision or choice -- provided that it falls within the parameters of what God has predestined!

Now that we have discussed predestination in chapter one and surveyed election in chapter two, it will prove helpful to review foreknowledge next. So, it is to a brief exploration of the meaning of foreknowledge that we now turn.

# CHAPTER 3: FOREKNOWLEDGE

## Definitions

Any examination of Calvinism must necessarily include surveying, and wrestling with, a definition of foreknowledge. Calvinist Loraine Boettner says that foreknowledge is the foresight of God concerning future events, asserting that divine knowledge is, therefore, unlimited, intuitive, innate, and immediate, being the eternal now of the divine mind.[79] Vine writes that the verb *proginosko* means to know before and is used of divine knowledge concerning Christ (1 Pet. 1:20), of divine cognition concerning Israel as God's earthly people (Rom. 11:2), of divine intelligence concerning believers (Rom. 8:29), of human knowledge of persons (Acts 26:5), and of human comprehension of facts (2 Pet. 3:17).[80]

Further, Vine also explains that the noun *prognosis* is used only of divine foreknowledge (Acts 2:23; 1 Pet. 1:2), is one aspect of divine omniscience, and involves God's electing grace, but does not preclude human will.[81] Notice once again that Vine takes a decidedly non-Calvinistic stance with reference to the human will. Arndt and

---

[79]  Loraine Boettner, "Foreknowledge," in *Baker's Dictionary of Theology*, ed. Everett F. Harrison, Geoffrey W. Bromiley, and Carl F. H. Henry (Grand Rapids, MI: Baker Book House, 1960), 225.

[80]  Vine, 459.

[81]  Ibid.

Gingrich simply say that foreknowledge is used with reference to God's omniscient wisdom and intention.[82]

## The Most Difficult Problem

The most difficult problem in this entire matter is reconciling foreknowledge with man's free agency and moral responsibility. Calvinism emphasizes God's sovereignty while Arminianism accentuates man's freewill. Scripture not only teaches the sovereignty of God in foreordaining and controlling events but also teaches the free agency and moral responsibility of man; and the Bible, some believe, makes no attempt to explain this mystery. Christian interpreters are, however, not left uninformed, for the incarnation paradigm, I believe, provides illuminating insights to several biblical enigmas. Just as the inspired Word of God posits both the divine and human natures of Christ Jesus, it likewise asserts both the sovereignty of God and the freewill of man. One consequence of the uniqueness of the nature of Christ is that no analogous parallels exist which can be employed *to explain* this riddle. As with Gen. 1:1 and its assumption of the existence of God - "In the beginning God...," explanation of these biblical paradoxes and their companion tensions is absent; yet, the fact of each paradox is assumed, though not explored, just as the fact of God's existence is presumed in Gen. 1:1, though untracked and unproven.

Hobbs argues that foreknowledge of an event does not cause it.[83] He further contends, rightly I think, that God never violates the human personality.[84] God knocks at the door of the heart, but will not force it open (Rev. 3:20). Foreknowledge, therefore, means simply that God knows but He does not violate human freedom and responsibility in any way. He knows all things, cares for each of His creatures and provides for each. A short discussion of God's providence, then, is next on our list to review.

---

[82] Arndt, 703-4.
[83] Hobbs, 67.
[84] Ibid.

# CHAPTER 4: PROVIDENCE

## Definition

No single word in Greek or Hebrew expresses the idea of God's providence.[85] J. I. Packer says that in Christian theology it is "the unceasing activity of the Creator whereby, in overflowing bounty and goodwill (Ps. 145:9; Matt. 5:45-48), He upholds His creatures in ordered existence, guides and governs all events, circumstances, and free acts of angels and men, and directs everything to its appointed goal, for His own glory."[86] As its root implies, God provides.

## Is to Be Distinguished from Isms

Packer also writes that providence is to be greatly distinguished from *pantheism*, which absorbs the world into God, teaching that everything is God; from *deism*, which cuts the world off from God; from *dualism*, which divides control of the world between God and another power, usually Satan, and tends to construct opposites in many categories; from *indeterminism*, which opines that the world is under no control at all; from *determinism*, which means control that destroys or eliminates man's moral responsibility; from *chance*, which denies

---

[85]  J. I. Packer, "Providence," in *The New Bible Dictionary*, ed. J. D. Douglas (Grand Rapids, MI: William B. Eerdmans Publishing Co., 1962), 1050.
[86]  Ibid., 1050-1.

that the controlling power of the universe is rational; and from *fate*, which denies that the controlling power is benevolent.[87]

Packer's definition of providence, however, is far too deterministic for evangelical Christianity to accept indiscriminately. While I certainly agree that God's providence includes His unceasing activity, overflowing bounty, goodwill, and the upholding of His creatures in ordered existence, I part company with Packer when he says that God's providence includes His guiding of *all* events and circumstances, including all the "free" acts of men and angels. What? God guides the free acts? But if God guides the free acts, how then are the acts free? Did God guide the revolt of Lucifer too? No He did not.

I think providence means that God governs and provides and that He is in charge and His objectives will be achieved. And this is done without violating man's freewill.

Now that we have completed these very abbreviated discussions of predestination, election, foreknowledge, and providence, it is time to turn our attention to Calvinism's concept of freewill. Since there is not much to say, I promise to be brief!

---

[87]  Ibid., 1051.

# CHAPTER 5: CALVINISM'S CONCEPT OF FREEWILL

## Acknowledges Human Responsibility Is Scriptural

Calvinist Cornelius Van Til, former Professor of Apologetics, Westminster Theological Seminary in Philadelphia, Pennsylvania, acknowledges that human responsibility is taught in Scripture, but he stresses that the meaning of human responsibility must be taken from Scripture itself and not defined or deduced from human philosophy.[88] This sounds fine, so far, but here comes the stumbling block, as I heard Sproul say, and it is that human responsibility must, then, relate to the all inclusive plan of God,[89] meaning that humans can do what they wish, but only within the confines of God's predetermined (all inclusive) plan. In other words, there are some things one simply cannot do and cannot "not" do. This means that one can only exercise one's freewill within the box, and, regarding salvation and election, one is certainly "free" to choose Christ *when one is elected to do so*, but not "free" to choose Christ if one is not elected to do so. What sort of freedom and responsibility is this when one is definitely not free to say "no" to God? Van Til further teaches that human responsibility takes

---

[88] Cornelius Van Til, "Calvinism," in *Baker's Dictionary of Theology*, ed. Everett F. Harrison, Geoffrey W. Bromiley, and Carl F. H. Henry (Grand Rapids, MI: Baker Book House, 1960), 109.

[89] Ibid.

place within history, and that history is under the ultimate disposition of God.[90] In other words, God is determining all things and man is free to act only as his actions *correlate* with God's *predetermined* plan (tell that to Jonah!). This, says Van Til, is the best way to understand that man is responsible as a creature of God.[91] So, Calvinism overtly teaches that man has a freewill, of sorts, but it can only be exercised within the parameters of God's will. Once God elects or does not elect, one's freewill can only be exercised within the confines of what He has elected. This model clearly contradicts the concept of freewill and choice, and results in no freewill at all.

## Seeks to Be Truly Evangelical?

Calvinism overtly appears, sometimes, to be truly evangelical in stressing the free offer of the gospel, at least Van Til thinks so.[92] But this sort of evangelicalism, says Van Til, is only true as it relates to the sovereign grace of God, for without relation to the sovereign counsel of God, there would be no human responsibility.[93] In other words, everything hinges on the sovereign counsel of God, which is true because the divine element must be acknowledged, but this view is grossly inadequate because it neither explains the extent of human responsibility nor takes this element more seriously. As we shall see in the upcoming section, the human will is at liberty to choose right or wrong. And it is at this point that we enter the heart of my critical review of Calvinism as we recognize first its strengths and then expose its many weaknesses.

---

[90]  Ibid.
[91]  Ibid.
[92]  Ibid.
[93]  Ibid.

# CHAPTER 6: STRENGTHS AND WEAKNESSES OF CALVINISM

## Strengths

The strengths of Calvinism include its emphasis on the sovereignty of God, its stress on God's involvement with and for man, and its accentuation upon the biblical teaching of the security of the elect (not the security of the believer, because faith is rendered basically useless in so far as it is preceded and preempted by regeneration in the Calvinistic paradigm), although Calvinism calls this the perseverance of the saints. The Bible undeniably teaches all of these things, asserting that believers are perfected for all time (Heb. 10:14), protected by the power of God (1 Pet. 1:5), and that believers shall not be disappointed (1 Pet. 2:6). Also, Calvinism justly promotes the biblical teaching regarding the sinfulness of man, rightly emphasizes the primacy of the role of Christ in redemption, emphatically insists upon the work of the Holy Spirit in salvation, justifiedly stresses the significance of ethical obligations for the redeemed, properly discloses that God does indeed elect some to service, and, perhaps most notably, Calvinism openly maintains a high view of the inspiration of Scripture. These strengths notwithstanding, Calvinism's weaknesses are far more numerous and flagrantly inglorious. I will now discuss the weaknesses in descending order from the greatest to the least, that is to say from the strongest argument to the weakest argument in terms of word content.

## Weaknesses

### 1. Inclusive Weakness

Scripture teaches that whosoever will may come to Christ in repentance and faith. As you are about to see for yourself, the Scriptures related to this doctrine are legion.

A Psalm of David teaches that the Lord responds to all who call upon Him in truth (Ps. 145:18) and that the Lord hears the cry of those who fear Him and promises to save them (Ps. 145:19). Jeremiah recorded God's words when He said that even heathen nations who repent and turn to Him can become His people (Jer. 12:16). Joel registered God's words when He said that whoever calls upon the name of the Lord will be delivered (Joel 2:32). These Scriptures accurately summarize the testimony of the Old Testament regarding "whosoever will."

Then, the New Testament champions this doctrine unmistakably, providing a plethora of scriptural testimony which harmonizes perfectly with the Old Testament witness. The words of Jesus declared that God says to no person "seek in vain," but "seek and you shall find" (Matt. 7:7). He promised that all who ask receive (Matt. 7:8). Notice that asking precedes reception. Man clearly has a role in the salvation event, and it is requesting the Lordship of Jesus Christ by faith coupled with repentance. Jesus guaranteed that He would confess before His Father in heaven everyone who confesses that He is the Christ (Matt. 10:32). Jesus also averred that all humans are more valuable than any animal (Matt. 12:12). He asserted that whoever humbles himself or herself in childlike faith to Himself is the greatest in the kingdom of heaven (Matt. 18:4). Jesus also taught that everyone who abandons all for Him, making Him his or her top priority, shall inherit eternal life (Matt. 19:29). Further, we read that the invitation to join the bridal feast is issued to all (Matt. 22:9). And, finally in the Gospel of Matthew, we learn that *whoever* humbles himself will be exalted (Matt. 23:12).

In the Gospel of Mark Jesus said that *whoever* does the will of God is His brother or sister (Mark 3:35). He also declared that *anyone* can come to Him through self-denial (Mark 8:34), and that *whoever* loses his life for the sake of Christ actually saves it (Mark 8:35).

In the Gospel of Luke we learn by way of angelic proclamation that Jesus brings great joy for *all* people (Luke 2:10). Moreover, Luke interpreted the ministry of John the Baptist to be a fulfillment of Isaiah's earlier prophecy that a voice in the wilderness would come announcing that *all* flesh shall see the salvation of God (Luke 3:6). This idea is echoed in the words of Jesus when He said that *everyone* who comes to Him and hears His words and acts upon them is as wise as a builder constructing his house on a solid foundation (Luke 6:47). Luke, like the other synoptists, repeated the words of Jesus which pledge that *any* who hear and *do* the word of God are related to Christ (Luke 8:21). Luke reiterated the words of Jesus which affirm that *anyone* can come to Christ (Luke 9:23), that *whoever* loses his life shall save it (Luke 9:24), that *everyone* who asks receives, that he who seeks finds, to those who knock the door shall be opened (Luke 11:10), that God's Holy Spirit is given to those who *ask* (Luke 11:13), that *everyone* confessing Christ is admitted into heaven (Luke 12:8), that *all* who deny Christ are denied access to heaven (Luke 12:9), and that, once again, *whoever* loses his life shall preserve it (Luke 17:33).

I love all of the books in the Bible but I have a particular fondness for the writings of John and Paul. John the Apostle wrote that John the Baptist came to witness to the light that *all* might believe (John 1:7). He also certified that as many as *receive* Jesus become children of God (John 1:12). John the Apostle even recorded the revelation from John the Baptist which asserted that Jesus is the Lamb of God who takes away the sin of the *world* (John 1:29). Jesus told Nicodemus that God loves the *world* and that *whoever* believes in Christ will not perish but have everlasting life (John 3:16). Jesus further explained to Nicodemus that God sent Him into the world to save all the *world*, not just some

(John 3:17), and that he who believes in the Son has eternal life (John 3:36). Jesus promised to grant eternal life to all who *ask* (John 4:10), and that all who hear and *believe* are given life (John 5:24). Clearly then, personal belief triggers the regenerating work of the Holy Spirit. Moreover, Jesus wants all to believe in Him whom God sent (John 6:29), and He promises that God gives the water of life to *all* who ask Him (John 7:37).

Luke recorded Simon Peter's explanation of what happened on the day of Pentecost. Peter saw Pentecost as a fulfillment of Joel's earlier prophecy (Joel 2:28-32) which announced that *everyone* who *calls* on the name of the Lord will be saved (Acts 2:21). Peter's racism and redemptive exclusivity required a special revelatory vision from God before the impetuous Apostle could finally see that God does not show partiality regarding salvation (Acts 10:34). Peter, therefore, preached that, in every nation, those who fear and do what is right, i.e., place faith in Christ, are welcomed by God (Acts 10:35). Then, Luke wrote concerning the converted Pharisee, Saul of Tarsus, whom we know as the Apostle Paul. Paul, in an early sermon, affirmed that through Christ *everyone* who *believes* is freed (Acts 13:39). Paul cited Isaiah (Isa. 42:6) in asserting that God wants salvation, not just the gospel, spread to the ends of the earth (Acts 13:47). In his sermon on Mars Hill Paul proclaimed that God has declared that *all* people *everywhere* should repent (Acts 17:30), pointing out that proof has been furnished to *all* men by way of the resurrection of Christ (Acts 17:31). Lastly, Luke provided helpful insight in this scriptural examination of Calvinism when he asserted that some were *persuaded* to believe in Christ but that others would not believe (Acts 28:24). Notice the presence of persuasion and personal belief, as well as the obvious fact that the situation was not that some could not believe, as if they were not part of the elect, but that they would not believe, which stresses personal accountability and rejection of the grace of God.

I admit that the Book of Romans is very challenging to understand. I have preached and translated through it word by word twice now and am somewhat tempted to write a commentary on it. But, for now, let me review several key passages which harmonize well with all the previous verses I have examined, and also dispel any notion that Paul taught the redemptive exclusion of any, except for those who exclude themselves through refusing to believe. He stated that the gospel is the power of God for salvation to *all* who *believe* (Rom. 1:16). This means that the gospel uniquely demonstrates God's power. The gospel of Jesus Christ is something of which to be proud, not ashamed. True Christians are those who are neither *ashamed* of the gospel nor a *shame* to it.[94] Are you ashamed of the gospel? Are you ashamed for others to know your hero and Savior is a Jewish carpenter who was executed as a criminal? Are you ashamed to follow Him in baptism? Are you ashamed to say you believe the Bible? Are you ashamed that doing so might damage your popularity? Paul shouted that nothing could turn him against the gospel! Conversely, I am ashamed of unchristian beliefs dressed up as Christian beliefs: infant baptism as washing away the taint of original sin; transubstantiation; the Mormon doctrine of becoming a god and populating one's own planet; and many of the claims of Calvinism. The gospel is the good news, and good news necessarily implies that "bad news" exists. The gospel is good news to receive, not a code to keep.[95] It is God's dynamic power and divine energy. Christians see God's power at work in lives and understand that one test of anything is to examine the results which are produced. The transforming power of the gospel is more than a theory; the gospel gets results. Christians are not powerless to change the evil in the world because the gospel is God's power to change lives, granting salvation to all who believe. The goal of the gospel is salvation. Salvation means deliverance from sin and its penalty and includes rescue from the wrath of God. In fact, the term "salvation" presupposes peril or danger from which humans

---

[94]  Matthew Henry, *An Exposition with Practical Observations of the Epistle of St. Paul to the Romans,* in *Matthew Henry's Commentary on the Whole Bible,* vol. 6, *Acts to Revelation* (McLean, VA: MacDonald Publishing Company, n.d.; reprint, n.d.), 367.

[95]  John William MacGorman, *Romans,* in *Layman's Bible Book Commentary,* vol. 20, *Romans - 1 Corinthians* (Nashville, TN: Broadman Press, 1980), 24.

need to be rescued.[96] The gospel is not the power of God for salvation to every person; Universalism is disallowed; it is the power of God for salvation to all who *believe*. All who believe may experience salvation, for Scripture teaches that *whosoever will* may come to Christ in repentance and faith: it is for everyone. Salvation is conditional upon belief, and saving belief means trust, personal commitment, handing over of one's self, and the wholehearted involvement in the truth being believed. Faith is believing obedience (James 1:22; 2:17). Personal responsibility to the gospel through faith is emphasized in Rom. 1:16.[97] Moreover, the equality of sinners and the equality of faith are stressed. By this I mean that if you are a sinner you can believe in Jesus Christ and be saved. The gospel is God's power to the Jews first and also to the Gentiles. Salvation is from a Jew (John 4:22) and began in Jerusalem among Jews (Acts 1:8). But it is also for Gentiles. Although the Jews were first in New Testament redemptive chronology, they will also be first in penalty (Rom. 2:9). The Bible is explaining that God's plan includes all of mankind, clearly announcing that it is the same salvation experienced by all. There is only one God, therefore, there is only one gospel and it is for all people.

In Rom. 3:22 Paul wrote that the righteousness of God is available through Jesus Christ as the object of faith to *all* who believe. Oddly enough, [sometimes] Calvinistic commentator Matthew Henry remarks that the righteousness of God, which is appropriated through faith in Christ, "is *eis pantas* - *unto all*, offered to all in general; the gospel excludes none that do not exclude themselves."[98] It would be difficult to find a more obvious reference to a general atonement in the works of an Arminian theologian! Is this "early" Henry or "late" Henry? Regardless of the age of Matthew Henry when he wrote it, this plainly appears to be a glaring inconsistency on behalf of a writer many believe to have been strongly Calvinistic (see Appendix A for more

---

[96] Ibid., 23.
[97] J. P. McBeth, *Exegetical and Practical Commentary on the Epistle to the Romans* (Dallas, TX: by the author, 1937), 42.
[98] Henry, *Romans*, 386.

of Henry's inconsistencies). I have read quite literally thousands upon thousands of pages written by Matthew Henry and my assessment of this statement is that he did not know what else to do with the verse. Although he is terribly given to an allegorical method of interpretation (hermeneutic), there was no way to take this verse except as it is officially stated in the Greek.

Romans 3:22 teaches that righteousness is imputed through faith in Jesus Christ. Righteousness is not imputed through works, baptism, or penance but through faith, and it is for all who believe. None who believe are excluded. So mankind is not saved for his faith but through it. Faith does not do the saving but it can and will appropriate the grace of Him who does the saving. Also, Paul argues that there is no distinction between people, thus indicating the universal condemnation of Jew and Gentile alike. Acquitting the innocent and condemning the guilty is the norm in man's courtrooms; but acquitting the guilty who believe in Christ and repent of sin is the norm in God's courtroom. Romans 3:22 teaches that the righteousness of God is imputed through faith in Jesus Christ for all who believe: this verse articulates the universality of the cure. Then, Rom. 3:23 follows by expressing the universality of the disease when it unconditionally proclaims that all have sinned and fall short of the glory of God. A universal shortfall demands a universal windfall and God has provided it in the person of Jesus Christ.

In Rom. 9:33 Paul wrote that *all* who *believe* in Christ will not be disappointed. When he said "it is written," he was probably alluding to Ps. 118:22, Isa. 8:14, or both. He was alleging that the Jews' own Bible predicts the offensiveness of Christ.[99] The Bible says that "God laid in Zion." This means that the plan of salvation was God's doing and the work of Christ was God's doing. What did God lay in Zion? A stone of stumbling. This declares that Christ was put here on earth, in a manger, in Nazareth, in Jerusalem, and on the cross by God. However, this does not mean that God caused stumbling. The Jews were advancing along on what they thought was a clear religious path and then they

---

[99]  C. K. Barrett, *The Epistle to the Romans* (New York, NY: Harper & Row, Publishers, 1957), 194.

tripped over what they deemed "debris" in the road. They stumbled over the necessity of faith in Christ as God's son and as the only way of attaining righteousness. This suggests that failure to utilize Christ Jesus as the foundation stone in life results in people taking offense at Him and stumbling over Him. The Jews were and are deeply offended by Christ. By His actions in reaching out to sinners, healing on the Sabbath, cleansing the Temple, and rebuking the Pharisees and scribes as hypocrites. They are also offended by his claims to be God's son and to be able to forgive sin. Further, they are offended by His demands of discipleship, of moral purity, of justice for all, and by His requirement of child-like faith. Still further, they are offended by His lowly birth and His scandalous death. Yet, in spite of all these actual and potential offenses, the Bible forthrightly proclaims that he who believes in Him will not be disappointed. This is speaking of a person and the person is Christ (Isa. 28:16; 1 Pet. 2:6-8). Those who choose not to trust Christ by faith will be crushed under the weight of their own sin and unrighteousness.[100] The rock sent to justify and deliver becomes the rock which judges and dooms. Thus, God is not to be blamed for any who are lost. Only those seeking to establish their own righteousness by the law of works stumble over Christ. Anyone who believes in Jesus Christ will not be disappointed.

In Rom. 10:13 Paul wrote that *whoever calls* upon the name of the Lord will be saved, something that Joel 2:32 had already announced. "Whoever" means that anyone can call upon the name of Jesus and be saved: liars, thieves, adulterers, prostitutes, drug addicts, alcoholics, murderers, atheists, Gentiles, Jews, black people, white people, tall people, short people, young people, old people, male people, female people, even church members! But they themselves (middle voice) must call. Scripture teaches both that Christ calls upon man and that man must call upon Christ and calling upon means invoke or appeal to, and

---

[100] Kenneth Boa, and William Kruidenier, *Romans*, in *Holman New Testament Commentary*, ed. Max Anders, vol. 6, *Romans* (Nashville, TN: Broadman & Holman Publishers, 2000), 307.

the appeal is to one name: Jesus (Acts 4:12). Those who call upon Him are saved, having been declared righteous and eternally secure.

And then in Rom. 11:32 comes a truly biblical theme which appears consistently in nearly every major contributor to Holy Writ: God wants to show mercy to all. This means that all unbelievers are looked upon in the same way. The Bible here definitively expresses the universal sinfulness of mankind. Both Jew and Gentile alike are confined within the scope of one kind of guilt, and it is that of unbelief.[101] Kenneth Wuest, former Instructor in Greek at Moody Bible Institute in Chicago, Illinois, interprets this to mean that by being shut up under disobedience, all are made to feel the need for grace.[102] This verse, then, teaches that every person must be damned before he or she can be saved. Here stands a double-barreled declaration: God classifies all accountable people as unbelievers and God wants to show mercy to all. God makes no ethnic distinctions. God makes no gender distinctions. God makes only a spiritual distinction: belief or unbelief. In that God desires to show mercy to all, we see the universality of sin: all people (Rom. 3:23; Gal. 3:22); and we see the universality of mercy: all people. Berkeley Mickelsen, former Professor of Bible and Theology at the Graduate School of Wheaton College, Wheaton, Illinois, asserts that God shuts up all for the purpose of setting all free.[103] Just as this text declares the universality of mercy and the universality of sin, it also asserts the universality of God's *invitation*;[104] but in no way does this verse teach the universality of salvation. Further, it is biblically inconsistent to suppose that Paul would argue for the universality of sin and then argue for the limited scope of its cure.

---

[101] Kenneth S. Wuest, *Romans*, in *Wuest's Word Studies*, vol. 1, *Mark - Romans - Galatians - Ephesians and Colossians* (Grand Rapids, MI: William B. Eerdmans Publishing Co., 1955; reprint, 1973), 201.

[102] Ibid., 202.

[103] A. Berkeley Mickelsen, *The Epistle to the Romans* in *The Wycliffe Bible Commentary*, ed. Charles F. Pfeiffer and Everett F. Harrison (Nashville, TN: The Southwestern Company, 1962), 1219.

[104] Dale Moody, *Romans*, in *The Broadman Bible Commentary*, ed. Clifton J. Allen, vol. 10, *Acts - 1 Corinthians* (Nashville, TN: Broadman Press, 1970), 246.

Paul's second epistle to the Corinthians maintains that Christ died for *all* (2 Cor. 5:15). Paul believed that Christians had been given the ministry of reconciling *all* to Christ (2 Cor. 5:18), not just a select group. Further, Paul echoed the words of Jesus found in John 3:16 when he wrote that God was in Christ reconciling the entire *world* to Himself (2 Cor. 5:19).

Paul's letter to the Colossians discloses that the Apostle pled with everyone he could to come to Christ (Col. 1:28). If language means anything, Paul taught *everyone* that he or she could come to Christ (Col. 1:28), and passionately desired to present *everyone* complete in Christ (Col. 1:28).

The writer of the Book of Hebrews said that Christ is the source of eternal salvation to *all* who *obey* Him (Heb. 5:9). In Heb. 12:15 the same writer admonished his readers to exhaust all resources to see to it that no one misses out on the grace of God. This insists that people pursue the grace of God. Evangelical Christians then must strive to see to it that nobody comes short of the grace of God, for we are our brother's keeper. To rely on one's own works is to come short of God's grace. The writer to the Hebrews knew well that to become aware of God's grace in Christ and still revert back to the Temple sacrifices would spell disaster. To rely on anything other than the *blood* of *Christ* is to come short of God's grace. God's grace is tall, man's works are short. God's grace is deep, man's works are shallow. God's grace is free, man's works are costly. God's grace brings cleansing, man's works leave filthiness. We must be active evangelistically such that we do all that is within our power to see to it that every person has the opportunity to experience God's grace. And it is plainly possible to *reject* God's grace. We must allow no root of bitterness to spring up, cause trouble, and defile because bitterness rots the bones. Bitterness, like sin itself, is contagious. We are herein told to uproot bitterness in our life. When the weed of bitterness rears its ugly head it poisons everyone around it. We must prevent this. Does this verse not demonstrate that God's grace is both resistible and accessible to all? I believe that it does.

Peter argued that the atoning work of Christ is for all of mankind and that Jesus is the Master who bought *all*, including unbelieving heretics (2 Pet. 2:1)! Further, notice that the false teachers bring destruction on *themselves* (reflexive pronoun) and others. This clearly implies personal accountability for choices, arguing against having been "destined" from eternity by God to be a false teacher.

In 1 John 2:2 John the Apostle insisted that Jesus is the propitiation for the sins of the *whole world*. Propitiation means satisfaction to the demand of God. His holy revulsion to sin demanded it and His loving grace provided it. God is the provider of salvation. Moreover, propitiation, in my estimation, is not appeasing an angry God, it is removing the cause for alienation.[105] John intended for his readers to understand that God does the reconciling in that He initiated it by providing Jesus. With the death of Christ, the cause of our estrangement from God, sin, is removed and the way of approach to God is made possible through union with Christ.[106] As the propitiation, He is available to atone for the sins of all believers and for the sins of the whole world. The scope of His work is all sin and all sinners. Christ's propitiation is effective for all, bringing life to whosoever will believe and death to whosoever will not believe, for God was in Christ reconciling the world unto Himself (2 Cor. 5:19). First John 2:2 is, quite simply, an obvious reference to a general atonement.

In 1 John 4:14 John echoed this same truth when he wrote that the Father sent the Son to be the Savior of the *world*. The apostolic witness of John and his colleagues is that they beheld Jesus Christ as the one sent by God the Father to be the Savior of the world. The apostolic witness is convincing because they were there and had been bearing witness to God's plan of salvation, even in the face of danger and death. They refused to be silenced and continued to proclaim that the Father had sent the Son. This sending by God speaks to His intentionality.

---

[105] Edward McDowell, *1-2-3 John*, in *The Broadman Bible Commentary*, ed. Clifton J. Allen, vol. 12, *General Articles, Hebrews - Revelation* (Nashville, TN: Broadman Press, 1970), 199.

[106] Ibid.

"Was sent," not "was created," declares the pre-existence of the Son, thus confessing the deity of Jesus Christ. And their confession was that the Son was sent to be the world's Savior. This means that He had a purpose and that purpose was to be the *world's* Savior. This affirms that every person is important to God. God wants all to receive Christ as Savior.

Later in his life the Apostle John wrote that the Spirit and bride say come to all and take the water of life freely (Rev. 22:17). He taught that anyone who hears, who is thirsty, and who wishes to drink of the water of life may do so.

We have seen, then, that God wants all to be saved and that Christ died for all, although this does not mean automatic, universal salvation is applied to all without personal faith and repentance. We have also seen that many remain unsaved, like the Pharisees of Paul's day and the false teachers of Peter's. Conclusively, then, they are unsaved due to their own rejection, not God's rejection of them. But some choose to receive Christ. Therefore, man is not so totally depraved that he cannot respond affirmatively to God's grace. Election is not unconditional, the atoning work of Christ is unlimited in its scope, and the grace of God is resistible.

Moreover, Calvinism misses the biblical point that election was always for inclusion rather than exclusion. God extended a call to Abram (Gen. 12:1). God intended to make Abram into a great nation (Gen. 12:2). God designed to bless Abram and make his name great (Gen. 12:2). God meant for Abram to be a blessing to others as well as to Himself (Gen. 12:2). God's selection of Abram was for the express purpose of blessing *all* the families of the earth (Gen. 12:3). Abram's exclusive selection always had an inclusive objective: all humans. God intended to enter the stream of history through Abram and redeem all the people of the world. Abram was elected to be God's primary ambassador. Abram was chosen to bring others to God and to take God to others. Therefore, these undeniable facts demand that any references to election be interpreted from the perspective that the elect are whosoever will, while the non-elect are whosoever will not.

The power of life and death rests in the work of Christ (John 17:3) and God gave Christ power over all humanity. God also presented Christ with the assignment of redeeming humanity, and Jesus did not fail. Christ purchased redemption for all humanity. I like to use an athletic illustration by saying that He "drafted" all, wishing to give eternal life to all, since He has been given all, but not all choose to sign with His "team." The elect are "whosoever will" sign with His team, while the non-elect are "whosoever will not." And, there is a major difference between will not and cannot. God made a way for all to come to Him, and that way is Christ Jesus. This offer of redemption is universal in its scope, meaning that it is for all of humanity. Nevertheless, this redemption must be appropriated individually by way of faith and repentance: no Universalism allowed. Redemption is not automatic. Mankind must respond individually. Alister McGrath asserts that the doctrine that Jesus died only for the elect is not found in the New Testament.[107] So, do God's standards vary between the "elect" and the so-called "non-elect"? Does God have any expectations for the "non-elect"? If there are expectations, what does it matter, if Calvinism is biblically correct, since they are destined to remain in their non-elect condition?

Calvinists seem to be theoreticians who rarely reflect upon the serious theological and anthropological implications their system of thought necessitates. As I state elsewhere, it would be ludicrous for Paul to argue so forcefully for the condemnation of the entire race (Rom. 3:9, 10, 11, 19, 22, 23) and then argue for a cure available only to a few. Paul had been a Pharisee and was the son of a Pharisee (Acts 23:6). Timothy Trammell says that Pharisees were the most prominent religious group of Judaism.[108] They were descendants of the interbiblical Hasidism and had crystallized into a distinct party by the time of the Hasmonean era (142-63 B.C.).[109] They placed emphasis on

---

[107] McGrath, *Justification by Faith*, 153.
[108] Timothy Trammell, "When John and Jesus Started Ministry," *Biblical Illustrator* (Winter 2000-01): 60.
[109] Ibid.

divine providence, but also recognized that individuals are *free moral agents* with choices to make.[110] If Trammell is correct, Paul's training as a Pharisee, then, would have led him away from understanding depravity, unconditional election, limited atonement, and irresistible grace as defined by Calvinism.

How do most evangelicals interpret the word "depraved," particularly with reference to the depravity of mankind as discussed by the Apostle Paul in Rom. 1:28? The Greek word Paul employs is *adokimos*, which is routinely translated depraved (NASV), base (RSV), and reprobate (KJV).

While word studies are necessary and helpful, they are rarely the final court of appeal when one is engaged in biblical interpretation, which, as I have been saying, is known as hermeneutics. Evangelicals have long championed the grammatical-historical method of interpretation, recognizing that word definitions are simply one of several integral elements to be included, along with other components, in order for sound interpretation to occur. Most would agree that the single most important element in the interpretive process is context.

Generally speaking, there are two schools of thought regarding human depravity. The first, that of Pelagius, says that mankind's mind was *damaged* as a result of Adam and Eve's sin. The second, that of Augustine and the Calvinistic/Reformed tradition, says that mankind's mind was not only damaged, but that it was also *destroyed* such that it became totally and incorrigibly unreliable as a result of Adam and Eve's sin.

John Newport, representing evidential apologetics and the dominant evangelical position, argues that humans can indeed grasp knowledge about God despite being hampered by finiteness and sin.[111] Conversely, Cornelius Van Til teaches that, because of the destructive effects of sin, unsaved mankind cannot understand the world as it really is. Even though God has shed His light throughout the created order, the minds of unsaved humanity are so radically darkened in

---

[110] Ibid.

[111] Newport, *New Age*, 601.

sin that they cannot see spiritual truth;[112] yet, he says, the Holy Spirit will enable the "elect," and only the "elect," to respond to the Gospel. On his own, man is so totally depraved, says Van Til, he cannot even respond affirmatively to God. This definition of depraved uses the word "totally" and means precisely that. Proponents of this view contend that mankind's reasoning capabilities were utterly destroyed, not merely damaged, such that God must do everything in order for one to be saved. He must even orchestrate the response of the individual.

As stated above, context is the key hermeneutical (interpretive) element. The paragraph of Rom. 1:24-32 clearly discloses that people, long after Adam and Eve, did not see fit to acknowledge God any longer (Rom. 1:28). "Exchanging" (Rom. 1:24) means they tested God at first and had knowledge of Him, but consciously rejected truth and enthusiastically received lies. A description such as this accurately summarizes an individual's life as one which *becomes* hardened by the deceitfulness of sin (Heb. 3:13). The heart does not start out this way. Paul concluded that intentional casting down of God in the mind (Rom. 1:28) results in depravity. This means that anarchy and chaos come from a mind that removes God from its knowledge. In estrangement from God, speculation displaces perception, and most are keenly aware that religious conjecture is legion in today's world. It is at this point that one is given over to do what is improper, and Paul unswervingly denounced homosexuality as improper (Rom. 1:26-27), citing this sinful activity as one classic example of depraved individuals who have been turned over to the darkness of unrestrained impulses.

Still, a depraved mind, even that which manifests itself in the vilest of ways, is not such that it cannot respond to God's grace. Van Til's concept of all people being born with his definition of a totally depraved mind due to Adam and Eve's sin simply does not square with the contextual definition presented by the Bible in this passage of Scripture. Depravity does not erase innate (inborn) knowledge of God, nor does depravity render one unable to respond to God's grace. While it is true

---

[112] Ibid.

43

that all have sinned and fall short of God's splendor and perfection (Rom. 3:23), and in this sense all have a mind damaged both by Adam and Eve's sin and one's own sin, the human mind is not destroyed such that it cannot respond with faith in Christ Jesus, thus accepting God's provision of grace. Sadly, though, many show no interest in God's grace until tasting of sin's disgrace. This is unquestionably the majority interpretation among evangelicals, regarding the biblical meaning of depravity.

From bumper to bumper, we have seen that God's Word expresses His focus of redeeming the world. Once the Bible has been consulted, it is obvious to see that Calvinism sports a terrible inclusive weakness.

## 2. Optional Weakness

Teachings espousing a limited freewill simply do not square either with Scripture or with life experience. Man does have options, both godly and ungodly (Prov. 1:29). Regarding election, Thom Rainer, LifeWay President and former Dean of the Billy Graham School of Missions, Evangelism and Church Growth and Associate Professor of Missions, Evangelism and Church Growth at The Southern Baptist Theological Seminary, says that anyone who is lost forfeits salvation because of his or her own disobedience, not because of election or predestination.[113] He acknowledges that a tension exists between humanity's freewill and God's sovereign choice, and, unlike some of his Calvinistic former colleagues at The Southern Baptist Theological Seminary, asserts that election is a sovereign, eternal decree from God which involves the *choice* of people to be the recipients of grace and salvation.[114] I am comfortable saying that if election is understood as to service, it is extended to some; but if election is understood as to salvation, it is extended to all.

I already briefly explored predestination. Rainer says it means to mark out beforehand, but rightly adds that this does not absolve

---

[113] Thom S. Rainer, *The Book of Church Growth: History Theology, and Principles* (Nashville, TN: Broadman & Holman Publishers, 1993), 140.
[114] Ibid.

humanity of the clear mandate to *receive* Christ and make disciples.[115] John Newport declares that one aspect of mankind being created in the image of God is the gift of reason, and with it the power of reasonable choice, that is to say the ability to decide for ourselves.[116] Fisher Humphreys, Professor of Divinity at the Beeson Divinity School of Samford University in Birmingham, Alabama, and former Professor of Theology at New Orleans Baptist Theological Seminary, argues that no Scripture should be interpreted to mean that God chooses any person for condemnation.[117] McGrath asserts that, like the invalid at the pool of Bethesda, mankind is given the privilege of accepting or rejecting God's cure for sin (John 5:6).[118] McGrath further maintains that it takes two to make a relationship, and unless man says "Yes" to God, that relationship remains unfulfilled, for God has given mankind the immense privilege of saying "No" to Him.[119] McGrath declares that God treats humans as persons, not as objects.[120] Conversely, rape involves treating a person as an object, which is exactly what both Calvinism and Universalism propose. Indeed, this is a repulsive analogy magnifying an outrageous tenet of each of these isms, neither of which is compatible with inspired Scripture.

A walk through the Old Testament demonstrates that mankind has a freewill and exercises it in every facet of human existence. Moses asserted this exercising of the freewill regarding choice of spouse (Gen. 24:5), contributions to God (Exod. 35:5), the offering of sacrifices to God (Lev. 1:3), and the presenting of peace offerings to God (Lev. 19:5). He again stated that sacrifices were offered according to the will of man (Lev. 22:19), and that thanksgiving sacrifices were offered at the will of man (Lev. 22:29). The inspired Chronicler proclaimed that God wants man to have a willing mind, but it is up to man (1 Chron. 28:9), and that God entreats man to consecrate himself, but man must

---

[115] Ibid.
[116] Newport, *New Age*, 440.
[117] Humphreys, 50.
[118] McGrath, *Justification by Faith*, 19.
[119] Ibid., 104.
[120] Ibid.

be willing (1 Chron. 29:5). Isaiah declared that man must be willing to obey God (Isa. 1:19).

Perhaps one of the most famous passages in all the Old Testament regarding human options and God's sovereignty is the one found in Jer. 18:1-12, which many recognize as the potter and the clay text. Jeremiah argued that both the potter and the clay are involved in shaping the clay into the vessel it will become. Moreover, this passage of Scripture may be the greatest text in the Old Testament for explaining the conditional nature of prophecies and purposes. While God's nature never changes, nor does He repent in the human sense, His purposes, quite obviously, can be altered according to the moral and ethical decisions of man.

Notice in Jer. 18:1-3 that God speaks through ordinary occurrences. The potter had a purpose in mind and it is good, not evil, because God is good and not evil (Jer. 18:3). No good potter designs bad vessels intentionally. Human options are available. Also, we know that it is not God's will that man murder man, nor is it God's will that man steal from man, neither is it God's will that man go to hell. Although man does not always choose to do so, the highest wisdom of man is to seek the potter's good purpose. But there is the possibility of perverting the potter's purpose.

Jeremiah 18:4-12 explains that the sovereign God works through free people. Man is free to choose sin or salvation (Jer. 18:4). The spoiling of the clay is not due to the potter's mistake. Any spoiling is due to the stubbornness of the clay as it resists the potter's touch, thus, man can resist God's will. There would be little use in praying "Thy will be done" if it were already happening. But, thankfully, the potter can remake the vessel (Jer. 18:4); however, in order to do so the potter must crush the clay and start over. Additionally, Jeremiah knew that the stubbornness of sin hardens and hardening brings wrath (Jer. 19:11). God's is a sovereignty that responds to the will of humans (Jer. 18:5-12). When He plans to pour out wrath upon people because of their evil, He alters His plans when they repent (Jer. 18:8). God remains willing to reshape the destiny of nations and individuals if they repent (Jer. 18:8). When He plans to bless, He alters His plans when they are disobedient (Jer. 18:10). God does not so much change His mind as He changes His plan (Jer. 18:8, 10). God's actions, then, are conditioned by the moral behavior of mankind. Prophecy is not causative but morally conditioned whether stated or unstated. Evil action forfeits the rights to the fulfillment of a promise. In the case of Israel, an obedient remnant would receive fulfillment of the promises. So, the unlimited power of God is exercised according to man's conduct not according to an unchangeable determination.[121]

Jeremiah further asserted that God does not afflict man willingly (Lam. 3:33). Daniel observed the freeness of the human will when he declared that the King of Persia would rule as he pleased (Dan. 11:3). And, Hosea announced that nations and people choose willingly to live as they do (Hos. 5:11).

Jonah 1:1-3 is another excellent Old Testament example of the exercising of the human will in direct opposition to God's revealed will. The Bible says that the word of the Lord came to Jonah (Jon. 1:1). We are not told how the word came. Was it audible, written, or was Jonah simply stirred from within? Regardless of the medium, Jonah knew what it was. Ironically, the historical drama of the prophet Jonah somewhat parallels the factual drama of the nation of Israel in that both the nation of Israel and the prophet Jonah had been selected for the task of delivering God's word to the world (Gen. 12:1-3). Jonah's resentment toward the all-inclusive scope of God's love reflects the narrow exclusivity of any who would restrict the range of God's saving grace only to an elect few. God wants to show mercy to all and He wants to bless all. Believers are told to go and be His witnesses, even to those who drove the nails into the hands of Jesus and to the one who pierced His side with a spear, that they all might repent and believe (Acts 1:8). Jonah is commanded - the words are imperatives - to *arise, go* to Nineveh, and *preach* against it (Jon. 1:2). The idolatry (fertility cult), self-confident pride (Isa. 10:13), and cruelty to others

---

[121] C.F. Keil, and F. Delitzsch, *Biblical Commentary on the Old Testament, Jeremiah,* by C. F. Keil, vol. 8. trans. James Kennedy (Grand Rapids, MI: William B. Eerdmans Publishing Co., reprint, 1986), 295.

(Nah. 3:1, 10, 19) practiced by the inhabitants of Nineveh had reached God's limit. In that Jonah was commanded to preach *against* the city, the threatening nature of the message becomes obvious. Jonah was to announce imminent judgment, leaving to the conscience of each listener to judge why it was coming.[122] When the cry of wickedness goes up to God, the cry of judgment comes down to man.

Nineveh was a principal city of Assyria (Gen. 10:11-12) whose oldest discovered remains date to ca. 4500 B.C.[123] Assyria had waned in military superiority but was regaining power. It was to these hated, oppressive people that God commanded Jonah to go and preach, some fifty years before Assyria's invasion of the Northern Kingdom in about 722-21 B.C. Jonah's assignment was not just for the good of Assyria but also served to shame Israel, in that a heathen nation would repent as a result of one sermon from one prophet, whereas Israel and Judah had heard many sermons from many prophets without repenting. However, even with the knowledge of God's will and the awareness of the spiritual needs of the Ninevites, Jonah fled from God's presence. He exercised his option.

Did Jonah really think he could escape from the presence of the Lord? No, he knew better, for in Jon. 1:9 he admitted that God was Lord of heaven, that God made the sea and the land, and fully believed that God was capable of destroying distant cities like Nineveh. "Fleeing from the presence of the Lord" is metaphorical language only. "Standing in the presence of the Lord" was also a figure of speech indicating a special position of service to God (2 Chron. 29:11). What a horrible thought: Jonah *chose* to resign his position as a prophet rather than be obedient. Jonah was attempting to escape his duty.

In all the other books of the prophets the reader encounters faithful men whose sole intent was to proclaim ardently the word of God which turns mankind to repentance, but not with Jonah, at least not

---

[122] H. L. Ellison, *Jonah*, in *The Expositor's Bible Commentary*, ed. Frank E. Gaebelein, vol. 7, *Daniel - Minor Prophets* (Grand Rapids, MI: Zondervan Publishing House, 1985), 369.

[123] Ibid., 368.

here. Voluntary obedience to the leadership of God is essential for the well-being of man. Nevertheless, God could have turned to someone else, but did not.

Jonah set out on a journey. To go to Nineveh? No way! Nineveh was only 500 miles northeast of Israel. He went toward the Palestinian coast to catch a ship headed to Tarshish! The human will can resist God's will. Ironically, some yearn to know the will of God in order to do it, while others already know the will of God and spurn it. Many Bible scholars think that Tarshish was in Spain, if so, this is the opposite direction (west) of where God told Jonah to go (east) and was as far away as he could get from God's will! Does going the opposite direction sound familiar? He put as much distance as possible between him and Nineveh, implying that he wanted nothing to do with the assignment and that he wanted as far away as possible from God's destructive action. He expected a God-bomb to be dropped on Nineveh and he wanted it to happen.

No one really knows for sure where Tarshish is, although most of us have been there - the exact opposite of what God wants! Jonah did what many do today when it comes to Christian responsibility - run, hide, or quit. Jonah found a ship headed opposite of where God wanted him to go and the Bible says he "paid the fare." What an understatement! Did he ever pay, and with more than money! He would pay dearly with endangering the lives of others, suicidal tendencies, the terror of darkness in a fish's belly, the stench of the same, and the damage to his body caused by the digestive secretions in the fish's stomach. Carnal (fleshly), renegade believers cannot rebel against God without incurring His disciplinary chastisement. Jonah "paid the fare" alright, and dearly. He boarded the ship in disobedience to God, being quite willing to suffer the inescapable vengeance of heaven rather than evangelize the Ninevites. He knew how hideously cruel and barbaric the Assyrians were in war, wrenching out the tongues of enemies, flaying people alive and then stretching out their skins on city walls to terrify and leave lasting fears. When he heard that Nineveh would be destroyed he leaped for joy! Jonah feared that God's mercy would spare the Ninevites, so he decided that he would rather die than have thousands of Assyrian converts. Jonah wished to escape, not beyond God's presence, but beyond God's service. The will of God was intolerable to him. Thus we poignantly learn that obedience to God demands renunciation of prejudices and of the lust for vengeance upon enemies, and requires letting the mind and will be shaped in accordance with God's mind and will. Jonah chose to refuse his God-given assignment and it almost cost him his life. Nevertheless, he had an option and he exercised it.

Further, Jon. 3:9-10 reiterates what we saw in Jer. 18 regarding God changing His plan in response to man's choices. The King of Nineveh was unsure how God might react to city-wide repentance. "Who knows?" he asked. "Perhaps God will turn and relent." "Maybe he will withdraw his burning anger so that we might not perish." The Ninevites were uncertain how faith and repentance would be received by God, whereas we know most assuredly the results these produce. But what happened? The answer is found in Jon. 3:10. The Lord spared Nineveh. God saw their deeds. Notice also that their repentance was demonstrated by deeds, not just by words. God saw that they genuinely turned from wickedness. Thus, God got what He wanted from them and no animal sacrifices were even necessary, only broken and contrite hearts. The Bible says that God changed His mind concerning the destruction He was about to bring. This means that God heaved a sigh of relief. His greatest desire is not to destroy man but to save him. Hence, God's actions are conditional based upon what man does or does not do. When we opt to repent, God is effectively relieved of His obligation to punish our sin and He is cleared to do what He longs to do - show mercy. God delights in showing mercy to the penitent. He can deal either gently or harshly with man, for both are in His repertoire. In Jon. 3:10 God rescinded His order of destruction because the people repented, thus God changes His mind as man changes his manners through faith and repentance.

So, both Jeremiah and Jonah underscored a significant fact about God: He is more concerned with moral and ethical responses than the literal fulfillment of promises, and will, in fact, alter those prophecies in accordance with man's behavioral choices which are borne out of faith and repentance. It is far better that Jonah be embarrassed over his prophecy not coming to pass than that a repentant soul be sent to hell! God offers man and woman a new start. You have only to turn to him in repentance, faith, and obedience! The Old Testament certainly declares that mankind has options and may choose them, even if they are not what God wills, but woe to those who opt to rebuff God.

A survey of the New Testament documents harmonizes beautifully with the testimony of the Old Testament concerning human options. Matthew recorded the words of Jesus when he taught His disciples to pray. Jesus stated that there is God's will and implied that there is man's will (Matt. 6:10). Jesus said that man may or may not choose to do the will of God (Matt. 7:21), that whoever does the will of God is related to Christ (Matt. 12:50), and that willingness to follow Him rests with man (Matt. 16:24). He further declared that the Father wills that none should perish, not one little child, which all of us begin as (Matt. 18:14). Jesus also implied that doing the will of God is optional when He taught the parable of the two sons (Matt. 21:31). And, I think one of the most fabulous of all passages regarding the human freewill is the one which relates the prayer of Jesus just before His arrest, in which is seen His human will conflicting with the will of God; but Jesus voluntarily submitted His human will to God's will when He said, "... if it is possible, let this cup pass from Me; yet not as I will, but as Thou wilt" (Matt. 26:39).

Mark recorded the words of Jesus as declaring that man can do good whenever he is willing (Mark 14:7). Luke announced that the birth of Jesus demonstrates God's good will toward all mankind [not simply the elect] (Luke 2:14). Luke further pointed out that killers exercise their wills, for Jesus was delivered by Pilate to the will of the mob (Luke 23:25).

The Apostle John noted that there is a distinction between the will of man and the will of God when he pointed out that those who are born again are not born of blood, nor of the will of the flesh, nor of the will of man, but of God, and we have already seen that God's will is for all to be saved and that none perish (John 1:13). This verse is not discounting the human element in salvation, for the previous verse has already asserted that the right to become a child of God is granted to as many as *receive* Him (John 1:12). Also, we see again that Jesus acknowledged the presence of His human will and God's will, and that He subjected His human will to God's will (John 5:30). Further, when Jesus discussed Peter's future with Him, He intimated that man can conduct his life as he wills, and he can change his will, as did Peter between his early rambunctious years and his later spiritually mature years (John 21:18).

Paul recognized that mankind struggles within between willing to do what is right and actually doing what is right. In Rom. 7:18 he wrote that nothing good dwells in man, but then amended his statement to say that nothing good dwells in one's flesh, probably implying that something good does dwell in one's spirit. To say that nothing good dwells in man is not a complete view of saved or unsaved man, as Paul shows by stating that to will to do good is present within him. The desire to do right is present within. The law of conscience is present in all. This consciousness of right and wrong has been damaged but not destroyed. Humans know the difference between right and wrong, but doing what is right is difficult and often unnatural. Paul knew that the sin nature is powerful and understood that there is a cataclysmic conflict between willing and doing. He taught that man can do what he wills, and in the context of 1 Cor. 7:36 it is regarding allowing a daughter to marry. Paul also saw that some have stronger wills than others (1 Cor. 7:37). Additionally, Paul stated that he acted voluntarily concerning preaching the gospel, and not against his will (1 Cor. 9:17). In the case of Apollos, Paul disclosed that he wanted Apollos to pay a visit to Corinth, but that Apollos' desire was not to do so right then. So we have here a reference to man's will concerning where to go and minister, and also when to go (1 Cor. 16:12). Paul even recognized that Satan has a will, and he tells Timothy as much (2 Tim. 2:26).

I do not know the name of the human agent God inspired to write the Book of Hebrews. What I do know is that he asserted that mankind can choose to sin wilfully (Heb. 10:26). He also admonished his readers to see to it that they not refuse (Heb. 12:25). Refuse God? Is this possible? Hebrews 12:25 declares that God speaks. As in the case of Jonah, we are not told how, so we are left to deduce that He does so through the conscience, through nature, through His spoken word, through His written word, and most excellently through the blood of Jesus Christ. Nevertheless, God can be refused. We all have a choice. First, there is truth. Second, there is knowledge of Christian truth making its appeal to the intellect. Third, there is faith, unable to prove or disprove the truth, venturing to act upon the truth. He wants all to receive Him, not refuse Him. God used prophets to warn people on earth. Prophets of God speak for God. Those rejecting the prophet or his words are actually rejecting God. Those rejecting the warnings of the prophets do not escape God's wrath on earth. Those rejecting God's warnings from heaven and turning their back on Him will not escape His wrath. See to it that you do not refuse God. This is the emphatic plea of the author of Hebrews. He employs a present imperative to urge his readers not to decline God's offers.

Simon Peter declared that shepherds (pastors), and others, can act out of constraint or willingly, meaning that we do have a will (1 Pet. 5:2). He also stated that no human will produces God's prophecy or Scriptures. There is, then, a clear distinction between man's will and God's will (2 Pet. 1:21). Further, Peter said that those refusing God's truth are willingly ignorant when they question the promise of Christ's return, in that they fail to notice that creation itself was begun at the word of God; thus, God's words regarding the return of Christ, which we have not yet seen, are as effective as His words which produced creation, which we have seen (2 Pet. 3:5).

The Apostle John did not cease his writing activities with his Gospel. In 1 John, he reported that man chooses to do the will of God (1 John 2:17). And in the Book of Revelation John affirmed that anyone who wishes may take of the cup of life (Rev. 22:17). The solemn invitation of Rev. 22:17 is that the Holy Spirit beckons all who hear or are thirsty to come. Then the bride says come, suggesting that

Christians beckon unbelievers to come to Christ. The one who hears says come, implying that those who know Gospel truth must invite others to come to Christ. The one who is thirsty may come. The one who wishes for eternal life may drink freely. The invitation is open to any and all. Revelation 22:17 is perhaps the most evangelistic verse in the book.

With J. W. MacGorman, I assert that, unless people are free to say "no" to God, neither are they free to say "yes" to Him.[124] Along these same lines, Marvin Vincent, former Baldwin Professor of Sacred Literature at Union Theological Seminary, New York, New York, writes,

> The potter does not make vessels in order to shiver them. God does not make men in order to destroy them. God ordains no man to eternal death. He desires to honor humanity, not dishonor it; and the fact that men do become vessels unto dishonor, merely proves the power which God has lodged in the human will of modifying, and in a sense defeating, His sovereign purpose of love.[125]

God but persuades, almighty man decrees. Calvinism has an appalling optional weakness which it cannot overcome from the pages of Holy Writ.

## 3. Restrictive Weakness

Doctrines referencing a "limited" atonement simply do not harmonize with the overall teaching of Scripture. Man is ordered to love God with all his heart, soul, and mind (Deut. 6:5; Matt. 22:37). This is a statement no one would deny. Therefore, since all are commanded to do so, it is necessary that all be *capable* of doing so.

---

[124] MacGorman, 27.

[125] Marvin R. Vincent, *The Epistle to the Romans*, in *Word Studies in the New Testament*, vol. 3, *The Epistles of Paul* (New York, NY: Charles Scribner's Sons, 1887; reprint, Grand Rapids, MI: William B. Eerdmans Publishing Co., 1980), 147.

One does not issue commands to unconscious entities, nor does one hold them responsible.[126] Man is conscious, and those who reach the stage of accountability are held responsible. Jesus said that God loves the entire world (John 3:16). Our Lord also declared that God desires for all of mankind to be saved, and this is recorded in the writings of several Apostles. Matthew recorded the words of Jesus when He disclosed that it is not the will of the Father that even one little child perish (Matt. 18:14), and every person begins as a little child. Likewise, John recorded the Gethsemane prayer of Jesus, which plainly published His desire that the whole world would believe in Him (John 17:21). Paul said the same thing when he wrote to Timothy and said that God desires that all people be saved and come to the knowledge of the truth (1 Tim. 2:4).

The context of 1 Tim. 2:1-7 has to do with instructions concerning prayer. The passage declares that there is one God, one Christ, who is the one mediator, and one target group: mankind. It further expresses that God cares for all; all should care for God; and all should care for one another enough to pray for all others. These instructions given by Paul to Timothy are intended to guide the church in its prayer life and conduct, for the measure of one's religion is reflected in the scope of his or her praying, and true Christian prayer must embrace the needs of all classes and conditions of men, beginning with everyone's need for salvation. Prayer is addressed first in Paul's discussion of worship because of its importance. Prayer for all (1 Tim. 2:1) is urged from every facet: entreaties, a word which intimates supplications for definite needs and suggests man's helplessness without God's aid; prayers, a general word suggesting reverence and worship; petitions, a word indicating freedom of access to God and reminding of the privilege of making requests for others; thanksgivings, a word instructing one to pray in steady, sustained ways, not just in times of crisis, to show gratefulness to God for the privilege of having access to Him at all times, and to thank Him for mercies already received. Paul told Timothy to pray on behalf of all

---

[126] John Wild, "The Present Relevance of Catholic Theology," in *Christianity and Reason* (New York, NY: Oxford University Press, 1951), 28.

others. Pray for those who may not pray for themselves, which includes sinners and saints. The fact of the matter is that there is nobody who is "not" worth praying for (double negative for emphasis). Moreover, these instructions to pray for all people remind that God wants all to walk in His light. Why would God instruct believers to pray for all people if He is not interested in redeeming and helping all? The answer is that He would not.

Next in order, Paul urged that prayer be made for those in authority (1 Tim. 2:2). He implied that this is to be done in order to help share their burdens. Paul said to pray for the leader, like Nero, not to him, because those in authority need to be saved too. He admonished Timothy and his Christian readers to pray for good rulers and bad ones as well. He would say to pray for the President, governors, and senators. He would agree that heavier responsibilities bring heavier needs and that we are less compelled to criticize those for whom we are earnestly praying and we will be more likely to recognize the heavy burdens resting upon their shoulders. He would say to pray that God will direct their decisions, which He will, and that they will follow His directions, which they often do not. Then, Paul listed the fruits of prayer for authorities: in order to live a quiet and peaceable life, because ungodly leaders make for disturbing days and restless nights; to live a godly life, because the better the leadership, the easier it should be to live in godliness; and to live an honest life, because the better the leadership, the easier it should be to be virtuous in all dealings.

Praying for those in authority pleases the Lord (1 Tim. 2:3). Praying for the salvation and the good of all people in general and authorities in particular pleases God. The Savior's nature is to rescue, not to condemn, so praying for the salvation and good of all is implied by the word savior. Christians must pray for the arch persecutors of the faith. As believers, we must pray for the salvation of all people and put feet to our prayers by modeling Christianity and by aggressively evangelizing the world. Clearly, this passage is a rallying cry for missions.

Next, we come to the heart of the message under consideration in this passage: God desires all to be saved and come to the knowledge of the truth (1 Tim. 2:4). The Greek text actually says that God wills *thelei* that all be saved. This is not teaching Universalism! On the contrary, the fact that all are not being saved suggests that God's will is being violated by man's will in the matter of individual salvation. But active responses of faith and repentance to God's grace are necessary. And, this wording is in the present tense. God is still willing all people to be saved. We, too, should be actively willing the same.

God does not desire the death or destruction of any human (Ezek. 33:11). Our prayers ought to seek to include all just as God's grace seeks to include all: inclusive prayer and inclusive salvation are clearly in context. We see that Christ died to save all people. This obviously expresses the theology of an unlimited (general) atonement. Also, understand that Jesus Christ died to save people, not pets or even angels, and that God has one divine purpose for all of mankind: to know Him personally and have fellowship with Him for eternity. God wants all people to have full knowledge of spiritual truth. Additionally, "to come" necessitates man's response to God's truth: people come freely and actively, not forcibly and passively. This stresses the necessity of evangelism and the fact that truth is found in Jesus Christ. Those who do not know truth cannot be ruled by it. Therefore, Christians must model, preach, teach, and write truth.

Further, Paul argued that there is only one God and only one mediator (1 Tim. 2:5-6). By teaching that there is only one God and one mediator the Bible is stating that the gospel of Jesus Christ is exclusive (1 Tim. 2:5). By stating that there is only one God the Bible implies that God intends good will to all, suggests the solidarity of the human race in terms of its common ancestry, teaches that the one God is common to all people, infers that the one God can reach all of mankind, asserts that only one God rules the universe, and takes for granted that salvation is available to all but originates from one source - the biblical triune God. Look carefully at this paragraph in the Bible and you will see the universality of prayer (for all people), the universality of God (one God for all people), the universality of God as the one mediator (one mediator for all people) who was enfleshed (the man) in the one

Christ (Jesus), and the universality of God in Christ Jesus as Savior (one savior for all people). Thus, the universality of grace, meaning that it is available to all, is rooted in the universality of God, who is accessible to all. This is not teaching Universalism! This is teaching the universal accessibility of God, His grace, and His redemptive activity. The insistence that there is only one mediator means that believers can mediate regarding prayers to God for others, but only one can mediate as the Savior. And, "mediator" presupposes that a controversy exists, that two sides are at odds. An intermediary must be able to identify with both groups. Only the God-man, Christ Jesus, can do this. There are no angelic mediators of redemption between God and man. There is no need for a priest, patriarchal saint, or a virgin mother. As Moses was the mediator of the old covenant, Jesus Christ is the mediator of the new covenant. Thus, the finite can enter into relationship with the Infinite by grace through faith and repentance.

As if the point had not yet been driven home, Paul proceeded to explain that this one Christ gave Himself as a ransom for all (1 Tim. 2:6), which echoes the very words of Jesus spoken in Mark 10:45. This indubitably teaches the doctrine of a general (unlimited) and substitutionary atonement, in that Christ Jesus gave Himself in exchange for all sinners. No other substitute would have been accepted. He paid the debt for all. He paid the penalty for mankind to gain freedom from sin and its wages and His entrance into the world and His exit therefrom were right on time.

Paul viewed himself as appointed (ordained) by God to be a herald of the gospel (good news), a special itinerant ambassador for Christ, and as a teacher who would labor in the word and in doctrine. He was called and commissioned by God, entrusted with interpreting the meaning of the Christian faith, had a personal faith in what he taught and preached, promised that he rendered a truthful representation of the Christian faith as he understood it, and even argued that he really was sent to preach and teach to Gentiles. No lie! People routinely ridiculed and challenged Paul's calling, ministry, methods, and authority. Today, people twist his words to say what he never would have said: that Jesus

Christ died as a ransom only for the elect and that God does not will the salvation of all.

There is plenty of scriptural testimony that Christ gave Himself as a ransom for all of mankind, not for a limited few. Isaiah said that the iniquity of us all fell upon the Messiah (Isa. 53:6). Peter even dared to proclaim that Jesus died for false prophets and heretics (2 Pet. 2:1)! This means that the ungodly were bought by the blood of Christ, regardless of the "degree" of ungodliness, for we are all miserable wretches in need of the Savior. I believe that these Scriptures sink the ship of a limited atonement theory. If Jesus died for false teachers, the implication is that He died for those who deny Him as Lord, meaning unbelievers who remain in their unbelief. The biblical fact that Jesus died for one who denies Him as Lord presents an insurmountable obstacle for belief in election and limited atonement as propounded by Calvinism because it says Jesus died only for the elect; yet, here are real people for whom Christ died. Jesus bought them with His blood. Since Christ died for false teachers and the teachers died unsaved, swift destruction having been brought upon themselves, the blood of Jesus was not shed only for the so-called "elect" but for all people. The doctrine (teaching) of a limited atonement is therefore scripturally indefensible. Unconditional election is therefore scripturally untenable.

Peter, like Paul, declared that God wants all to come to repentance (2 Pet. 3:9). Therefore, He is the potential Savior of all of mankind, but the actual Savior of believers only. John the Baptist announced that Jesus is the Lamb of God who takes away the sin of the *world* (John 1:29). Lest you, or anyone else, slide down the slippery slope toward Universalism, Paul reminded in 1 Tim. 4:10 that Jesus was the [potential] Savior of all, but especially of *believers*. Good servants labor and strive to spread this trustworthy statement, and the work of the servant is arduous. He explained that good servants fix their hope on the living God and announce the scope of God's saving plan. Jesus is the *potential* Savior of all but the *actual* Savior only of believers in Christ. His grace is *adequate* for all who will believe but *effective* only for all who do believe. He stands ready to deliver all. None are outside the scope of God's saving plan; His way is inclusive, not exclusive; He is the only hope people have; He is the source of all blessings and kind providence. The only barrier to salvation lies in each unbeliever's refusal to repent of sin and receive Christ as Savior.

In Titus 2:11 Paul wrote that salvation had been brought to *all* of mankind. He said that God's grace has appeared, bringing salvation to all. Grace is undeserved love, unmerited favor, and is absolutely free, for it cannot be earned. It, grace, has appeared at a definite time. This epiphany was a historical occurrence. Once hidden, now God's grace is revealed, and the best explanation for this revelation is that it is a reference to the incarnation (first coming) of Jesus Christ. The human situation was very bleak until God's grace appeared. God's grace arrived bringing salvation to all, not to a select few. But notice carefully that salvation was *brought*, not *applied*. The purpose of God's grace is to *bring* salvation to all. Redemption, then, is universal in its scope, since the Bible teaches that Jesus gave Himself as the ransom for all (1 Tim. 2:4). Clearly, Paul's words teach a general atonement (Jesus died for the sins of the world), not a limited atonement (Jesus died only for the sins of the elect). All are invited to partake, even those who hated and crucified Jesus. God's grace was disclosed for all to see (2 Tim. 1:10) and is available for all to receive, but God's grace is not automatically applied. It is set before every person like a Christmas present and left there waiting to be opened by way of personal faith and repentance. Salvation has been brought to all, not applied to all, for God violates no one's conscience.

The writer of Hebrews declared that Jesus tasted death for *everyone* (Heb. 2:9). This means that Jesus is the factor that makes all the difference. The writer said that Jesus was made, for a little while, lower than angels. But why? Because the suffering of death allowed Him to be crowned with glory and honor, because the suffering emphasized His humanity, and because the Savior must identify with the people He intends to save. He had to be a sufferer. Use of the word "death" in the verse emphasizes the fact that His experience went well beyond suffering, it concluded in crucifixion. Death defeated man but not the Son of Man. In the Son of Man's victory over death He made a mockery of it and opened its door. Thus, He is rightly crowned or rewarded with glory and honor. Note carefully the paradoxes: He was made lower than angels but given authority over all things; He was crowned with glory and honor in reward for sacrificial humiliation; and in Jesus, God stepped from *eternity* into *time*, and he did so for all sinners, including me. In some mysterious way, the grace of God allowed Jesus Christ to taste death for everyone. This was part of God's plan for redemption. Christ tasted death, He experienced it, for all. None are excluded except those who exclude themselves. Jesus died on your behalf. His sacrificial death is sufficient for all but only efficient for all those who repent and place faith in Him.

The writer of Hebrews also explained that Jesus is the source of eternal salvation to all who obey Him (Heb. 5:9). He was made perfect. He was tried severely and proven to be without blemish. This perfection advanced Him to the final completeness of the goal fixed by God. He had reached the end of the fleshly road and His obedience extended even unto death on a cruel cross. He graduated from the University of Physical Life with honors. And through His perfection, suffering, death, and resurrection He became the source of eternal salvation. Not *a* source but *the* source, to *all* those who obey Him. Notice the condition. No universalism allowed. Salvation is conditioned upon the loyalty of faith in Christ alone. And observe that the salvation He offers is eternal. Calvinism has an insurmountable restrictive weakness.

## 4. Revelatory Weakness

Calvinism does not seem to account for the fact that God has promised to reveal Himself in one way or another to everyone. Many Scriptures bear clear testimony to this fact. Isaiah said that people will see what they had not been told, and will understand what they had not heard (Isa. 52:15). The Apostle John announced that the true light enlightens every man, suggesting that God's redemptive scope is inclusive (John 1:9). The Apostle Paul proclaimed in Rom. 1:19 that what is known about God is evident within man. This means that knowledge of God is innate. God makes Himself known in them, that is in the human consciousness.[127] The present tense verb "it is" denotes the permanency of this knowledge of the personal God. Moreover, God has stamped knowledge of Himself once for all time upon human consciousness, which is denoted by the past (aorist) tense verb for "manifested."[128] No human being has ever been without this knowledge. This implies that one has the ability to know, thus eliminating infants and the mentally challenged. All people have received at least *general revelation within* and, with the exception of infants and the mentally challenged, are accountable for it.

Romans 1:20 declares that the truth about God is evident without. This means that divine truth about God as Creator, Judge, and Redeemer is evident outside each person. The *invisible* attributes of God's character are *seen* in creation through the medium of nature. Note carefully the paradox - the invisible is seen. How are these unseeable attributes observed? Through the heavens, the expanse, and through day and night God's glory is declared (Ps. 19:1-4). And God's care is proclaimed by way of rains and fruitful seasons in order to feed man and provide gladness (Acts 14:17). What is clearly seen is that God is God and that no created thing in the universe is God. God's eternal power is seen through creation, for things that are made cannot make themselves. He has the might to make something out of nothing (fiat creation). God's divine nature is seen through creation and the Creator transcends the creation. So, the existence of something as tremendous as the universe demands a Being of eternal power and divine attributes.[129] That Being deserves worship and total allegiance. The result of this knowledge and manifestation of truth is that mankind is without excuse for rejecting God and for falling into sin. God is the revealer and nature is the medium of his self-disclosure. However, His disclosure does not guarantee a positive response from people, yet it

---

[127] Moody, 170.
[128] J. P. McBeth, 52.
[129] Wuest, *Romans*, 30.

establishes the minimal ground of human responsibility.[130] Moreover, it is terribly imprecise to say that nature reveals God, for it is only the medium through which God reveals Himself. In other words God reveals, nature does not; nature is merely a medium.

Further, all people have received at least *general revelation without* and, with the exception of infants and the mentally challenged, are accountable for it. Therefore, our responsibility before God is based upon our response to the disclosure that God has made available to us.[131] Those who have general revelation are accountable for responding in faith to the biblical triune God who provides the general revelation. Yet, mankind suppresses, restrains, or holds back, meaning he refuses to obey the truth. Observation of created life sufficiently demonstrates that creation does not provide the keys to its own existence.[132]

Also, Rom. 10:18 explains that Israel had plenty of messengers and many special revelations from God. Thus, all receive general revelation. All have heard of God. The voices of the prophets go out into all the earth and their words extend to the ends of the world. Hearing is not the problem. Heeding is the problem. Knowing is not the issue. Responding to the light one has is the issue. Israel is without excuse, and so is the world

Then, in Rom. 15:21 the Bible teaches that Paul wanted to reach out to those who had heard no specific news of Christ. Paul wanted to impart understanding to those unaware of the gospel and he viewed his work as fulfillment of Isa. 52:15, which he cited. Isaiah's words suggest that those who have no news of Christ shall see and understand. However, God is not obligated to work through people, He may work through angels or simply through His Holy Spirit, but He will reveal Himself. It is a privilege to be allowed to participate in God's redemptive activity. The evangelistic work of man is an honor granted by God, not a right. He does not need us, yet He has opted to let us take part in revealing Him and His word to the masses.

---

[130] MacGorman, 26.
[131] Ibid.
[132] Barrett, 35.

63

All of this revealing implies that a decision either for or against Him, the Revealer, must be made by everyone, otherwise, why reveal? I am compelled to agree with the assertion that "around every soul there swirl the winds of sin and grace."[133] Further, I believe that, if indeed there are those who were never privy to the gospel message, due either to infancy, retardation, or insanity from birth forward, Jesus becomes "proxy" (not proxy faith but proxy person) for them and they will be admitted into heaven. In support of this view, remember the tragic case of the death of David and Bathsheba's son conceived as a result of adultery. King David said that he will go to his deceased infant son (2 Sam. 12:23). Now, David could have meant that he would join his son in the grave. But he could have meant heaven too, which suggests that the baby went to heaven, because David was certainly headed there, and David was declaring that he would go to his son. I believe God has made a way for Jesus to become "proxy" for those who never reach a stage of accountability, although much debate will surely be had determining what constitutes accountability.

The Bible teaches that he or she who hears (understanding is implied) becomes accountable, not he or she who does not hear (John 5:24). Hearing leaves man without excuse (John 15:22). So, because God has revealed Himself, His Word, and His Son, the accountability and the response of mankind to God's revelatory overtures are bound up in God's disclosures. In other words, God is not playing some cosmic game, revealing the necessity of faith and the redemptive work of Jesus Christ, without also simultaneously establishing levels of accountability on behalf of the recipients and eliciting their response. Calvinism does not do justice to the point of God's revelatory activity, therefore, Calvinism has a flagrant revelatory weakness.

## 5. Deterministic Weakness

Calvinism seems to share affinities with a Hindu caste system (see the comparison chart in Appendix B), which all evangelical Bible

---

[133] Clark H. Pinnock, *The Scripture Principle* (San Francisco, CA: Harper & Row, Publishers, 1984), 176.

scholars would reject outrightly. Like Hinduism, Calvinism basically opines that people are born into one of two castes: elect or non-elect. Moreover, virtually nothing can be done to change the situation; yet, Rom. 1:18 categorically denies the doctrine of inability, asserting, rather, the opposite position.[134] This text argues that people resist the truths of God, not that they are so depraved that they are unable to obey them. The passage declares that Gentiles had suppressed the truth about God (Rom. 1:18-20). In verse 18, Paul argues that the wrath of God is *revealed* from heaven. This revealing implies that God can be known. God is knowable because He reveals much about Himself through historical activity. Incidentally, this effectively refutes *agnosticism*, the teaching that knowledge of God cannot be known. Moreover, as J. W. MacGorman says, disclosure of God's righteousness delivers *from* sin while disclosure of God's wrath delivers *to* sin.[135] Similarly, the revelation of God's wrath also reveals His righteousness: see what angers Him, stop it, and go the opposite, righteous direction. God's wrath is His inherent reaction to sin. Only an impotent god would not be angry with sin, and, believe me, the one true God has zero tolerance with sin. His wrath is being revealed through His abandonment of people to the consequences of their sinful *choices*.[136] God's wrath is the same toward all ungodliness and unrighteousness. His ire cannot be resisted, but His grace can be. Besides, God's wrath is not some peevish display of bad temper but is His relentless opposition to all that would destroy His creation,[137] and humans are his creation. God seeks to dissuade people from their sin by handing them over to the consequences of their wickedness.[138] Notice that the Bible says that the revelation of God's wrath is against all ungodliness and unrighteousness. This means that God's wrath is against those suppressing the truth in unrighteousness,

---

[134] Louis Gifford Parkhurst, Jr., *Principles of Liberty: More Great Themes on Romans from the Writings of Charles G. Finney* (Minneapolis, MN: Bethany House Publishers, 1983), 33.

[135] MacGorman, 25.

[136] Ibid.

[137] Ibid.

[138] Ibid.

not against those who have never reached *accountability*. Babies and the mentally challenged are not guilty of ungodliness, unrighteousness, or suppression of truth. The accountability of the individuals referred to herein by Paul must be understood. This universal condemnation does not include those who never reach the stage of accountability (2 Sam. 12:23). I believe that God has made a provision for them in Christ. Those who never reach the stage of accountability have no comprehension of God's revelation and are, therefore, not accountable. But Paul's inspired words intimate that mankind knows better than to commit immorality and live in a state of irreligiousness: all knowers are guilty. Truth, when unrestrained, quickens one to activity and obedience, and resistance to truth brings hardening of heart.[139]

If Calvinism's views of election and predestination are correct, why does God wait until later in life on so many before saving them? Is this why infant baptism becomes so essential in the Calvinistic theological system? You might be surprised to know that reincarnationists avoid the giving of invitations, publicity, or advertisement, and simply trust the "Law of Attraction" to draw their own to them and them to their own.[140] Calvinism certainly shares some affinities here. The caste systems, then, become nothing more than mediums for propagating human prejudice and notions of elitism dressed up in religious garb. Racism is the dogma that one ethnic group is condemned by nature to hereditary inferiority and another group is destined to hereditary superiority.[141] Likewise, Calvinism is nothing short of "baptized racism," advocating the dogma that one group, the non-elect, is condemned by God to spiritual inferiority and another group, the elect, is destined to spiritual superiority. I do not intend to imply that Calvinists are racists. I am attempting to draw enlightening parallels between Calvinism, racism, and the caste system honored by Hinduism. All three share

---

[139] Parkhurst, 33.

[140] William Walker Atkinson, *Reincarnation and the Law of Karma: A Study of the Old-New World-Doctrine of Rebirth, and Spiritual Cause and Effect* (n.p.: Yogi Publication Society, 1908), 108.

[141] Foy Valentine, "The Contemporary Racial Crisis: A Christian Perspective," *Southwestern Journal of Theology* (April 1965): 20.

numerous common denominators (see Appendix B). Hence, the term "baptized racism" denotes the presence of prejudice, though not racial, in the spiritual realm: spiritual bigotry, if you will. Racism determines the ins from the outs by skin color; Hinduism determines the ins from the outs by birth into a caste; and Calvinism, or more properly Calvinism's view of God, determines the ins from the outs by election. All three fail miserably at acknowledging the presence of the image of God inherent in every human, making each person of inestimable value. All Calvinists are not racists but have many Calvinists embraced what amounts to "spiritual racism" because it is a more comfortable "Christian" philosophy which allows for the seemingly natural human propensity toward some form of individual superiority, allegedly predetermined by God? It would be interesting to know how many non-caucasians actually embrace five-point Calvinism as a genuine Bible doctrine.

Similarly, Calvinism and "Charismania" are deep ditches of opposite extremes located on either side of the narrow road of truth when it comes to their theologies.[142] Calvinism, with its emphasis on predestination, makes God the puppeteer and man the puppet. "Charismania," with its emphasis on prosperity theology, makes man the puppeteer and God the puppet. The sovereignty of God element in Scripture never suggests man's helplessness, nor does it threaten man's freedom of responsibility. Letters to the seven churches in the Book of Revelation show that the writer, the Apostle John, believed that man's decisions and responses in the world definitely shape history and personal destiny.[143] Conclusively, then, biblical Christianity invites those who do not like how they were born to be born again. Calvinism has a sordid deterministic weakness.

---

[142] I am indebted to Preston Nix, Pastor of Eastwood Baptist Church in Tulsa, Oklahoma, and a Ph.D. graduate in evangelism from Southwestern Baptist Theological Seminary in Fort Worth, Texas, for this assessment, which was related in a personal conversation 5 August 2002.

[143] Morris Ashcraft, *Revelation*, in *The Broadman Bible Commentary*, ed. Clifton J. Allen, vol. 12, *General Articles, Hebrews - Revelation* (Nashville, TN: Broadman Press, 1970), 245.

## 6. Christological Weakness

Calvinism verbally *affirms* that Jesus is 100 percent God and 100 percent man, but frequently *denies* that Jesus inherited a sin nature from Mary. But, be reminded that Mary had an Adamic sin nature too. The sin nature is not obtained from either one parent or the other, it is part and parcel with being human. Adam and Eve were not created with a sin nature but were created with a freewill. In the exercising of their freewill, each chose sin. Specifically speaking, Adam's transgression alone tainted every human being ever born thereafter with a damaged, though not destroyed, will. One born with this capacity is born with the nature. This theological fact, that Jesus had an Adamic nature, makes His sinlessness all the more remarkable and His atoning work perfectly efficacious (effective).

Some Calvinists with whom I have conversed teach that sin was an absolute impossibility for Jesus. Proponents say that man's sin nature is passed through the father, not the mother. Christologically (the doctrine of the nature of Christ) speaking, this virtually denies the humanity of Christ and all that is to be communicated through the title "Son of Man." If sin had not been a possibility with Jesus, then what was accomplished through His living of a sinless life? The Bible teaches that, in order for Christ to be the unique arbitrator, He had to identify in all ways with man (Heb. 2:17-18). The Bible also asserts that He was tempted by Satan himself to sin (Matt. 4:1-11), invited to indulge in the lust of the flesh (Matt. 4:3-4; 1 John 2:16), the pride of life (Matt. 4:5-7; 1 John 2:16), and the lust of the eyes (Matt. 4:8-10; 1 John 2:16). He hungered (Luke 4:2) and said that no one is good except God (Luke 18:19). Are these not references to His humanity? Are these not references to the nature He inherited from Adam? Moreover, the Bible says that He, unlike God the Father, fell asleep (Luke 8:23), bled (Luke 22:44; John 19:34), sweated (Luke 22:44), grew weary (John 4:6), and thirsted (John 4:7; 19:28). And, perhaps most persuasively, John said that "the Word became flesh" (John 1:14). This is the climax of the previous thirteen verses in the opening chapter of John's gospel, and may be the most important verse in the entire Bible. The Godhead is Spirit, not flesh. Nevertheless, God the Son accepted living in a frail human body. He had never before been limited to time, space, matter (body), or finiteness. In using the word "flesh" (*sarx*), John teaches that God the Son took on human flesh, which is called the "incarnation." Before the Word could be fully exalted, He had to be limited. What meaning can one extract from the words "became flesh" apart from the Virgin Birth? Christ, who created flesh, now became it. The Word did not enter a man, dwell in a man, or fill a man; the Word became a man. Christ assumed a human body and took on man's nature in its totality. He is no mere semblance of God or man, He is literally God and man. God the Son did not merely clothe or veil Himself in flesh, He became flesh, entering into a new mode of being, formerly only divine, but now both divine and human, perfectly fused in one man -Jesus Christ. God the Son did not simply assume a human body, He also assumed human nature too, and this is capably expressed by John's use of the word *sarx*.

While it is true that God the Father can neither die nor sin, evangelical Christianity believes that God the Son did die and could have sinned, but never did err, not in anything (Heb. 4:15). Jesus never missed the mark (1 Pet. 2:22). He became the perfect sacrifice for all sin and for all sinners. Further, there were things which God the Son did not know but that God the Father did know (Mark 13:32), another way in which the Bible expresses the humanity of Jesus.

Calvinism emphasizes the deity of Christ at the expense of compromising His humanity and further clouds the distinctions between Father, Son, and Spirit. Heresies that have been condemned in the past as unorthodox include Ebionitism, which emphasizes the humanity of Christ at the expense of His deity, arguing that Christ was a man born naturally upon whom the Holy Spirit came at His baptism.[144] This, by the way, is the Christology of Jehovah's Witnesses. A second Christological heresy, called Apollinarism, is quite similar to Ebionitism. A third is called Docetism. It emphasizes the humanity

---

[144] Ronald S. Wallace, "Christology," in *Baker's Dictionary of Theology*, ed. Everett F. Harrison, Geoffrey W. Bromiley, and Carl F. H. Henry (Grand Rapids, MI: Baker Book House, 1960), 120.

of Christ at the expense of His deity, saying that the humanity and sufferings of Christ were apparent rather than real.[145] A fourth is called Arianism, and it emphasizes the oneness of God at the expense of distinctions within the Godhead, proposing a basic denial of the Trinity by asserting that no divine emanation (like the Holy Spirit) can make contact with the world and further argues that Christ had no human soul.[146] Similarly, it is worth noting that a Monothelite is one who holds that Jesus Christ has but one will - the divine one. This doctrine was condemned as a heresy by the Sixth General Council (Constantinople) in A.D. 680. It takes its name from *monon*, the adverb and adjective meaning alone or only, and *thelo*, the Greek verb meaning I will, wish, desire. Likewise, George C. Fry, James R. King, Eugene R. Swanger, and Herbert C. Wolf, in their text *Great Asian Religions*, call belief that Christ had only a divine will and not a human will a "heresy." They cite the Maronite Church, the Eastern Rite branch of Roman Catholicism, as a denomination which "has flirted in the past" with this teaching.[147] Calvinists who deny that Jesus had a fully operable human will capable of sinning are unwittingly resuscitating, or clinging to, the monothelite heresy.

To be sure, perhaps not all Calvinists adhere to a Christology which demeans the humanity of Jesus; but some do. First Corinthians 15:45 teaches that Jesus represents all of humanity as the "last Adam." This speaks of the solidarity of humanity and Christ's inclusion therein. Complementarily speaking, then, Col. 2:9 declares that in Him dwells all the fullness of deity. This means that Jesus Christ is fully God. The heart of the heresy in Colossae, as with modern heresies, had to do with the nature and essence of Jesus Christ. Paul stated that all the fullness of deity dwells in Him and he used a common pre-Gnostic and later Gnostic word *pleroma*, the word of the heretics, for fullness. By it they probably meant elemental spirits, but Paul asserted that the

---

[145] Ibid.

[146] Ibid.

[147] George C. Fry, James R. King, Eugene R. Swanger, and Herbert C. Wolf, *Great Asian Religions* (Grand Rapids, MI: Baker Book House, 1984), 193.

real fullness was not found in a series of unseen powers but in Christ. The fullness of deity was not scattered but wholly concentrated in Jesus Christ, who is the essence and nature of the Godhead (*theotes*). Like John, Paul understood that God became flesh and dwelt among us and that Jesus is 100 percent divine and 100 percent human. Paul argued that Jesus was not simply *like* God, he was *fully* God in a body. God became man, man did not become God.[148] Such a declaration strongly opposes the false teaching that matter is evil by asserting that God indwelt human flesh in a bodily or material reality. While the image of God is found in every human, God Himself is found only in Jesus. In that Jesus represents all of humanity as the last Adam and that in Him dwells all the fullness of deity, this incarnate expression of God's righteousness has been placed at the disposal of all of mankind. Jesus Christ is the only virgin born person ever, is completely divine and fully human, and is, therefore, absolutely unique. Calvinism has a frightening Christological weakness.

## 7. Imago Dei (Image of God) Weakness

There are four basic views concerning mankind being created in the image of God: the substantive-structural view, the relational view, the functional view, and the composite or eclectic view. Let us briefly discuss these perspectives and their implications.

The *substantive-structural* view says that being created in God's image means that humans possess an inherent characteristic, or characteristics, be they physical, psychological, or spiritual, within our nature which include reason, self-consciousness, or self-determination.[149] The biblical passage used to support this view is Gen. 1:24-28.

The *relational* view says that being created in God's image means the experiencing of relationships, either between oneself and God or

---

[148] Max Anders, *Colossians*, in *Holman New Testament Commentary*, ed. Max Anders, vol. 8, *Galatians, Ephesians, Philippians, & Colossians* (Nashville, TN: Broadman & Holman Publishers, 1999), 319.

[149] Robert V. Rakestraw, "The Persistent Vegetative State and the Withdrawal of Nutrition and Hydration," in *Readings in Christian Ethics*, vol. 2, ed. David K. Clark and Robert V. Rakestraw (Grand Rapids, MI: Baker Book House, 1996), 125.

between human beings.[150] The *relationship* is itself the image of God. The biblical passage used to support this view is Gen. 1:26-27.

The *functional* view says that being created in God's image is something humans do, not something we possess, and this functionality is most commonly suggested by "rulership" or "dominion" over creation.[151] The biblical passage used to support this view is Gen. 1:26.

The *composite*, or what I call the *eclectic*, view is my favorite, and is probably the best, since it has the advantage of being a combination of the strengths of the previous three.[152] It has the broadness to include reason, self-consciousness, and self-determination with the depth to include the capacity for relationships with God and others, for doing and rulership, as well as including the mental and spiritual elements. W. R. Estep, longtime Professor of Church History at Southwestern Baptist Theological Seminary in Fort Worth, Texas, believes that to say that God created some for damnation and others for salvation is to deny that all have been created in the image of God (Gen. 1:26-27).[153] Additionally, *The Baptist Faith and Message* states, "The sacredness of human personality is evident in that God created man in His own image, and in that Christ died for man; therefore every man possesses dignity and is worthy of respect and Christian love."[154] This confessional statement challenges the Calvinistic definition of total depravity, the doctrine of unconditional predestination for some while others are left without hope, and the belief in a limited atonement. John Newport argues that the biblical worldview teaches that Israel's God is the Creator of all people from all nations and that the biblical worldview takes into account that all people in some sense start in the same place.[155] Likewise, the Book of Amos suggests that God's choosing

---

[150] Ibid.

[151] Ibid., 126.

[152] Ibid.

[153] William R. Estep, "Doctrines Lead to 'Dunghill' Prof Warns," *Texas Baptist Standard*, 26 March 1997, 12.

[154] *The Baptist Faith and Message* (Nashville, TN: The Southern Baptist Convention, 2000; reprint, 2003), 10.

[155] Newport, *New Age*, 49.

of Israel did not diminish His concern for other peoples (Amos 9:7). To be created in God's image includes the following assertions: (1) mankind is created for a special relationship to God; (2) mankind can make decisions; (3) mankind can respond to God's claims; (4) mankind is created as a rational and creative creature; (5) all of mankind are created for fellowship with God, as evidenced by the "Our Father" phrase in the Lord's prayer (Matt. 6:9); (6) mankind is created for eternal life with God; (7) mankind is created for dominion over the rest of creation; (8) mankind is created for social relations; (9) mankind is created as one human race; (10) there is only one human race; (11) and the human race is created as finite.[156] We must acknowledge that all humans have been made in the same image by the same Creator, all humans are created equally, and, therefore, partiality relative to salvation is not of God, as is evidenced in the charge of Moses to the judges in Israel (Deut. 1:17). God Himself is impartial regarding His created beings (Deut. 10:17). Humankind is definitively presented as indivisible in terms of race or skin color.[157]

Regardless of the view you take, we can all agree that when we sin, we disgrace this image. Being created in God's image undoubtedly includes being God's representative on earth. Whether a believer or an unbeliever, all humans exist throughout life as "imagers" of God, for all humans are made in God's image (Gen. 9:6). No other creature, including angels, can claim this wondrous distinction. Therefore, all humans are invaluable to God, being worth much more than birds, for whom He also cares (Matt. 6:26-30). All humans are said to be made in the likeness of God (James 3:9), and, as such, we are representatives of the king as His vice-regents on earth. I believe that being created in God's image presupposes some capacity for self-awareness and self-direction. Moreover, the scriptural idea of man being created in the image of God also means that mankind is called upon by God to bear

---

[156] Newport, *Christian Doctrine*, 88-90.
[157] Ibid., 90.

witness in his existence to God's existence.[158] It is likewise exciting to know that being created in God's image means continuing to live beyond the grave, as Boyd Hunt so capably points out.[159] This means that all humans are created for eternity. Everyone is going to live forever, the only question is where -- heaven or hell. God loves all humans unconditionally (John 3:16). His love wills the perfection of the loved ones: for God so loved the world [all humanity]. But, being created in the image of God does not make salvation automatic, it simply invites all to share in divine suffering,[160] for genuine saving faith necessitates dying to the self by being crucified with Christ (Gal. 2:20). Calvinism has a severe weakness regarding the doctrine of the Imago Dei (image of God).

## 8. Evangelistic Weakness

The notion of God choosing not to make salvation available to people through "election," thus leaving them in their sinful condition and its penalty of condemnation, clashes with scriptural teaching which states that Christ did not come to destroy lives but to save them. Such a "gospel" delivers no "good news" at all to lost sinners. We learn from Ezekiel that God inspired prophets to warn the wicked (Ezek. 33:8-9). The text shows that the prophet could choose to obey God and warn the wicked, or the prophet could opt to disobey God and not warn the wicked (another excellent text arguing for the freewill of man!). Whether warned or unwarned, the impenitent wicked would die in their iniquity, but God would somehow require the blood of the unwarned from the hand of the disobedient prophet who refused to warn them. This implies that God did not want the wicked to die in their iniquity and suggests that they could do so, even though God did not want them to die in the grip of sin. This text also suggests the

---

[158] Helmut Kuhn, "The Wisdom of the Greeks," in *Christianity and Reason*, ed. Edward D. Myers (New York, NY: Oxford University Press, 1951), 153.

[159] Boyd Hunt, *Redeemed! Eschatological Redemption and the Kingdom of God* (Nashville, TN: Broadman & Holman Publishers, 1993), 253.

[160] Alister E. McGrath, *The Mystery of the Cross* (Grand Rapids, MI: Academie Books by Zondervan Publishing House, 1988), 120.

responsibility of the messenger to speak and of the listener to obey. This is, indeed, a compelling passage for promoting evangelism. Be reminded that Ezekiel was sent primarily to the chosen people; yet, they could die in their iniquity, chosen or not. We further learn from Ezekiel, as pointed out earlier, that God takes no pleasure in the death of the wicked, but desires that all people repent (Ezek. 33:11). Additionally, Jesus proclaimed that the Son of Man came not to destroy, but to save (Luke 9:56). And, we saw earlier that John the Baptist testified that Jesus is the true light, that all might believe (John 1:7).

The universality of mankind's sinful condition demands the universality of the available cure, which must be personally appropriated. With Newport, I assert that, this side of heaven, nobody can be exempt from the possibility of redemption.[161] With this understanding of what it means to be created in the image of God, therefore, W. R. Estep charges that Calvinism's God resembles Allah, the God of Islam, because he is malevolent.[162] But, make no mistake about it - the biblical triune God, unlike the God of Islam, is benevolent, not malevolent.

I truly believe that Christ and Satan are locked in a cosmic struggle for the affections and souls of mankind. This fight is not restricted only to some group called the elect. Satan's targets include all of mankind. He wants to kill, spiritually and physically, the whole world. C. S. Lewis, longtime Professor of Medieval and Renaissance Literature at Cambridge University in Cambridge, England, says, "There is no neutral ground in the universe: every square inch, every split second, is claimed by God and counterclaimed by Satan."[163] Newport insightfully asserts that Satan's main objective is to frustrate the redemptive purposes of God.[164] Conversely, and thankfully, Christ Jesus refuses to concede any, but rather, fights for all.

---

[161] Newport, *New Age*, 49.
[162] Estep, 12.
[163] C. S. Lewis, *Christian Reflections* (Grand Rapids, MI: William B. Eerdmans Publishing Co., 1967), 33.
[164] Newport, *Christian Doctrine*, 97.

Now, stay with me here. By virtue of the fact that Satan desires to rule all, not just some, Christ also desires to rule all, not just some. If there are those "elected" for salvation and others "elected" (or left) for destruction, why would there be a cosmic battle? Over whom would the war be waged, since, if Calvinism is correct, everyone is accounted for? But, since there is obviously a war over souls which is raging, everyone is not accounted for; hence, the need for deception on behalf of the enemy, who would blind the hearts of all (2 Cor. 4:4), even the elect if he could (Matt. 24:24). The Bible openly states that the devil snatches away the word from the unsaved so that they will not believe and be saved (Luke 8:12). Estep argues that, logically, Calvinism is anti-missionary, and should rationally view evangelistic efforts as nothing more than exercises in futility.[165] This rationale, as Estep and others point out, contradicts The Great Commission (Matt. 28:18-20).[166] History bears witness that this evangelistic contradiction has frequently led adherents not to extend invitations for the lost to be saved at the conclusion of services.[167] Estep writes that Andrew Fuller penned *The Gospel Worthy of All Acceptation* against the Calvinism of John Gill. Fuller noted that, "Had matters gone on but a few years, the Baptists would have become a perfect dunghill in society." Estep further concludes that it was Fuller's modification of Calvinism among Particular Baptists that paved the way for the foreign mission movement of which William Carey, labeled by John Ryland, Sr. as "a miserable enthusiast," became the catalyst.[168] Estep then reports that London pastor John Gill was proud of the fact that he never extended an invitation for a sinner during his more than fifty years of ministry there.[169] What a tragedy.

Calvinism simply does not deal adequately either with the corporate or universal relatedness of mankind as a whole. This inadequacy

---

[165] Estep, 12.
[166] Ibid.
[167] Ibid.
[168] Ibid.
[169] Ibid.

severely undermines any theology of evangelism, which is certainly a biblical mandate not intended to be done merely out of obedience, as many Calvinists do, but out of a fervor to persuade men, women, boys, and girls to turn from sin and to Jesus Christ. Calvinism has a deplorable evangelistic weakness.

## 9. Theodical Weakness

I remember hearing from one of my seminary professors how a very close friend of his had been electrocuted while working on an air conditioner. After the funeral, many of the man's closest friends gathered at his home for food and fellowship. During this time, several of the men commented that it must have been God's will for the man to die, to which the rest agreed; except for my professor. He told us that he had listened to about all of this nonsense that he could stand and he finally spoke up and boldly asserted, "I think it was probably not God's will that he work on the air conditioner with it plugged in." The silence in the room was deafening.

Too often, God gets blamed for what He did not cause. Let me explain, from Scripture, the best biblical representation I have ever seen regarding causes of death. The text is 1 Sam. 26:10, which, I believe, does a marvelous service of describing three primary sources which can bring about death to people. These three are acts of God, acts of nature, and acts of man.

David was on the run from King Saul, who, in his madness, was intent on killing Israel's future king. In one particular encounter, David's military companion, Abishai, was sure that God had orchestrated things such that David would be Saul's executioner and effectively end this fiasco once and for all. But, again and again, David wisely declined to kill the troubled king. Instead, David explained to Abishai that there were at least three causes of death for man. My exposition of David's words is both an attempt to use them to help explain the problem of evil and suffering in the world and an attempt to defend the righteousness and goodness of God, which is known as a theodicy, hence, my categorization as a theodical weakness.

The first thing I notice that David said concerning death is that the Lord may strike one down. This I describe as an act of God. Such an act suggests the direct divine intervention of God in a matter. Usually, this sort of death is seen to be punitive. The chilling examples of Nadab and Abihu (Lev. 10:1-3) as well as Ananias and Sapphira (Acts 5:1-11) are biblical accounts which appear to fit the category of death being orchestrated by a direct act of God.

The next possibility that David mentioned is that Saul's day will come that he dies. This suggests death by way of what I call an act of nature (see also Num. 19:16, 18). No direct divine intervention is mentioned. No divine punishment is implied. The deaths of Abraham (Gen. 25:7-8) and Jacob (Gen. 49:33) serve as biblical examples of those who simply die of natural causes. Heart attacks, strokes, and other causes related to aging and worn out bodies fit into this category. Usually, tornado, hurricane, and flood victims also fit into this category, although I readily acknowledge the fact that evil powers may use nature to kill, as can be seen in the case of Job's family (Job 1:18-22). I also believe that the number of deaths by way of natural causes can be reduced by using caution regarding eating habits and taking cover when storms arise.

The third statement David makes is quite intriguing. David asserted that Saul may go down in battle. This I label as a death being caused by an act of man. One may be killed in battle, killed in a car wreck, killed in a shooting, and so forth. The biblical examples of the deaths of Saul (1 Sam. 31:1-4) and Uriah (2 Sam. 11:14-17) illustrate death brought about by an act of man. Similarly, some diseases can be traced to man, like AIDS, tobacco related cancer, radiation (sun) exposure, and more. And, I once again acknowledge that evil powers may use people to kill people (Job 1:13-17).

Not everything that happens is caused by God. There are acts of God, acts of nature, and acts of man. We would do well to remember these categories when it comes to explaining evil and suffering in the world. God is good and has man's best in mind; yet, the human mind and demonic forces seek to raise a barrier between God and man by questioning the goodness of God and making Him responsible for all evil and suffering, when He in fact has allowed man to sow what he wishes. But with sowing also comes reaping. Man wants to sow evil and then blame God for reaping suffering. The true culprits are people and demonic forces. Faith in Jesus Christ can protect us from demonic forces, but what will protect us from us? We must cease saddling God with all the ills of the world and assume the responsibility for our own demise. David clearly described three different possibilities and refused to lump them all together as acts of God, so neither should we. Calvinism has no answer other than "the sovereignty of God in predestination" when it attempts to explain causes of death. Such a defense is lame as well as blasphemous, in that it is shallowly ambiguous, untrue to Scripture, as I have sought to demonstrate in 1 Sam. 26:10, and is an affront to the righteousness of Almighty God. God (*theos*) is righteous (*dike*) and in Him there is no unrighteousness. These two Greek words brought together render the transliteration theodicy, or, more precisely, "Godrighteous." Calvinism has an appalling theodical weakness.

## 10. Repentance Weakness

Strict emphasis on the work of the Holy Spirit and minimization of the response of man disarm the importance of the biblical teaching of repentance.[170] The word *metanoia* means a change of mind, heart, and direction on behalf of the individual in response to God. Who would deny that Jesus came to call sinners to repent? The Bible teaches that He came to save what was lost, this means the unrepentant (Matt. 18:11). Jesus said to His listeners that they too would perish, unless they repent (Luke 13:3). He came calling sinners to repentance (Luke 5:32). All have sinned (Rom. 3:23). Therefore, Jesus calls all to repentance.

---

[170] This is reflected somewhat in the controversy between the "free grace" and "Lordship theology" schools of thought regarding soteriology. See Millard J. Erickson, "Lordship Theology: The Current Controversy," *Southwestern Journal of Theology* (Spring 1991): 5-15.

Newport smartly notes that, by definition, sin is a free and responsible act of disobedience and is man's *fault*, not his *fate*.[171] He argues that the New Testament description of God's judgment on sin clearly teaches that each human is accountable to God for the use of his or her freedom.[172] God's justice makes all of us accountable for our choices. God does not force His will upon anyone. He invites people to respond. Each person has an option.

Calvinism does not seem to factor in Scripture which teaches that it is not God's will that any should perish but that all should come to repentance. And the Bible is replete with evidence regarding this.

Through Ezekiel, God said that He takes no pleasure in the death of the wicked, but wants us to turn (repent) and live (Ezek. 18:23). In the same chapter, God urged all to repent and live (Ezek. 18:32).

Daniel exhorted Nebuchadnezzar to repent in hopes of avoiding God's "beastly" sentence upon the king's pride (Dan. 4:27).

Jesus said that it is not God's *will* that any little ones perish (Matt. 18:14). We all begin as little ones. Therefore it is not God's *will* that any perish.

Paul declared that all people everywhere should repent (Acts 17:30) and that God wants to show mercy to all (Rom. 11:32). Peter said that God does not wish that any perish, but that all to come to repentance (2 Pet. 3:9). In 2 Pet. 3:9 God's promise of Christ's return in judgment is balanced with His desire that none perish, but that all come to repentance. Here, Peter warned that mankind develops a mistaken sense of security, like a thief that has yet to be caught. God's longsuffering is due to His love for the lost, not due to any tardiness. His delay in the second coming is due to His mercy. God quite literally wants all people to repent and believe (1 Tim. 2:4). One of the strongest contrasting conjunctions, *alla*, is employed to stress God's desire that all repent instead of perish. Indeed, some will perish, as is seen in 2 Pet. 3:7, but this is not God's desire. Nevertheless, only the repentant and acceptant are saved (John 3:16). God's provision of grace is available to all who

---

171 Newport, *Christian Doctrine*, 99.
172 Ibid., 152.

*repent* and *believe*: repentance is seen here as indispensable, and perhaps even synonymous with, faith. The unrepentant, which is synonymous for unbeliever, will perish. This does not mean cease to exist, but to be banished to eternal torment where worms do not die and fire is not quenched (Mark 9:44-48), where judgment is eternal (Heb. 6:2), where the punishment of fire is unending (Jude 7), where torment in the Lake of Fire is forever and ever (Rev. 20:10-15). Moreover, Wuest says that God is always willing to save man, but man is not always willing to be saved by God.[173] Some do perish. So whose *will* causes the perishing? Newport rightly argues that it is not God's will but man's which results in one perishing.[174] Newport wisely declares that Christians need to explain to others that the basic tension in the biblical worldview is not between God's love and justice, but between God's will and man's will. He argues that man has chosen to assert his will against God's will, and, in so doing, man has alienated himself from God, from his own welfare, and from salvation. Newport further contends that God allows for man's autonomy to result in eternal separation from Him, but that God does not wish that anyone be eternally sequestered from Him; the choice is left up to each individual.[175] Thus, man is not so totally depraved that he cannot respond to God's grace. Election is not unconditional. Man has a will. The atoning work of Christ is not limited only to the elect. God's grace is resistible. Some opt to receive Christ and some, tragically, do not.

By not allowing for a freewill (truly free) and by asserting that regeneration precedes faith, Calvinism wrongly bypasses the biblical teaching of repentance as part of, or preparatory to (remember the ministry of John the Baptist), conversion to Jesus Christ. This repentance (metanoiaical) weakness is embarrassing.

---

[173] Kenneth S. Wuest, *2 Peter*, in *Wuest's Word Studies*, vol. 2, *Philippians - Hebrews, The Pastoral Epistles, First Peter - Jude* (Grand Rapids, MI: William B. Eerdmans Publishing Co., 1954; reprint, 1973), 71.

[174] Newport, *New Age*, 600.

[175] Ibid.

## 11. Response Weakness

Calvinism does not place enough responsibility upon the believer and the necessity of his or her response to God's grace.[176] W. R. White, who occupied the Chair of Missions at Southwestern Baptist Theological Seminary from 1923-1927 and served as president of both Hardin-Simmons University and Baylor University, contends that Southern Baptists belong to the Calvinistic wing of Christianity regarding their concept of salvation, but calls it a "modified Calvinism." He further explains that there are distinct points of departure from other denominations of this classification (Calvinistic), namely a personal faith as opposed to a parental or proxy faith. Also, White points out that Baptists reject the Arminian emphasis upon salvation by works. He concludes that Baptists are distinctive in their concept of salvation, differing from both Arminians and Calvinists, although retaining elements in common with each.[177] The term "modified Calvinism," then, suggests that most Southern Baptists retain terms like "total depravity," but define its meaning so as to exclude any idea of a mind so tainted by sin that it cannot respond to the grace of God. Like-minded evangelicals understand that some things are "predestined," like the death of Christ on the cross, but refuse to build our doctrine of salvation, regarding each individual and every event in each life, on the idea of an "unconditional predestination." Evangelicals recognize the concept of "election," but do not believe it violates the will of the person, nor do we believe that election constitutes automatic salvation. We reject any notion of a "limited atonement" and an "irresistible grace." And, we redefine the concept of the "perseverance of the saints" as the security of the believer, since not all the elect of Israel were believers. The term "hyper-Calvinism," then, would necessarily arise to describe basic five-point Calvinists, particularly those who follow Calvinism's tenets to their logical conclusions. White further argues that there are two essential reactions on man's part: repentance and

---

[176] W. R. White, *Baptist Distinctives* (Nashville, TN: Convention Press, 1946), 22.
[177] Ibid., 19.

faith.[178] For evangelical Christians then, regeneration does not precede repentance and faith, it follows it.

Additionally, Calvinism emphasizes the role of the Holy Spirit at the expense of the role of the person, teaching that salvation is 100 percent the activity of God and 0 percent the activity of man. But, with Herschel Hobbs, I contend that election is best understood as God taking the initiative in salvation and leaving man free to choose.[179] While most would agree that even the grace to believe, sometimes called prevenient grace, is supplied by God, few would concede that man has no role whatsoever. Many Scriptures reiterate the necessity of a personal faith, and it is clearly expressed with a possessive pronoun, "*Your* faith has saved you," (*he pistis sou sesoken*). Three examples uttered by none other than Jesus Himself can demonstrate this: "Your faith has saved you" (Matt. 9:22); "Your faith has saved you" (Luke 7:50); "Your faith has saved you" (Luke 8:48). If Greek grammar means anything in interpretation, and it does, then these *possessive* pronouns clearly indicate that the faith originates within the person in response to God's disclosures and results in salvation, not vice versa, as Calvinists claim when they teach that regeneration produces saving faith.

Therefore, it is incumbent upon mankind to repent, meaning turn to the Lord Jesus and away from sin (2 Cor. 3:16). The Apostle John reminded his readers that the victory which overcomes the world is "our faith," (*he pistis hemon*) (1 John 5:4), another possessive pronoun. It is this sort of faith, which is the substance of things hoped for and the evidence of things not seen (Heb. 11:1), that constitutes man's response, or role, in the salvation event. Thus, salvation, like the incarnation paradigm, is something that is both 100 percent a divine activity and 100 percent a human activity. Understanding the necessity of the human and divine elements, then, requires seeing that they cannot be regarded as an either/or proposition, but as a both/and

---

[178] Ibid., 22.

[179] Herschel H. Hobbs, *1-2 Thessalonians*, in *The Broadman Bible Commentary*, ed. Clifton J. Allen, vol. 11, *2 Corinthians - Philemon* (Nashville, TN: Broadman Press, 1970) 266.

declaration. In other words, salvation is not either a divine enterprise or a human enterprise, it is both a divine enterprise - God's grace offered to man through His call - and man's response with his own personal faith. The wonderfully insightful Southern Baptist theologian and longtime Professor of Theology at Southwestern Baptist Theological Seminary, Boyd Hunt, reminds that the Bible never teaches that God works and there is nothing for man to do; it teaches that God's work enables man's work (Phil. 2:12-13); God's grace is never intended as a substitute for man's responsibility.[180] Contrastingly, personal faith has little if any role in five-point Calvinism, which constitutes a notorious response weakness.

## 12. Theological Weakness

The Old Testament teaches that the Lord is one (Deut. 6:4) and the New Testament asserts that the Lord is one (Rom. 3:29-30). The biblical triune God is the God of Jews and Gentiles (Rom. 3:29). Since God is one, He is to be the God of all people. The way of salvation is equally suited to the whole family of fallen man. The universality of *justification*, meaning salvation is available to all people, is based upon the *unity* of God.[181] God justifies by faith and through faith (Rom. 3:30). God justifies the circumcised by their faith, meaning on the grounds of their faith.[182] God justifies the uncircumcised through their faith, meaning through the agency of their faith. In both instances faith is the cause of God's declaration of justification.[183] The same God who saves the Jew also saves the Gentile who places the singular instrument, *faith*, in the singular object, *Christ*. Thus, in declaring the oneness of God the Bible maintains the universality of God. The one and same God is Creator of all; however, He is not the Father of all, for the Bible declares that unbelievers have the devil for a father (John 8:44).

---

[180] Boyd Hunt, "The Person and Work of the Holy Spirit: The Effecter of God's Purpose" (Seminary Hill Station, Fort Worth, TX: by the author, 1989), 60.

[181] J. P. McBeth, 125.

[182] MacGorman, 46.

[183] Mickelsen, 1193.

Nevertheless, God wants to be the Savior of all. The Bible also teaches the inter-relatedness of humanity (Prov. 22:2; Rom. 3:23, 29, 30). This means that all of humanity are as one and God is one. This same God intends for Jesus to be the Savior of every person (Deut. 6:5, 13; Phil. 2:9-11); yet, five-point Calvinism essentially denies the universality of God, the solidarity of humanity, and the possibility for every tongue to confess Jesus Christ as Lord in this lifetime, and thus be redeemed. As J. W. MacGorman, my former New Testament professor on the Book of Romans at Southwestern Baptist Theological Seminary in Fort Worth, Texas, used to say, justification by faith affirms the universality of God.[184]

Let me try to explain this: God is one, and since God is one He is the God of all people. The universality of justification, meaning salvation is *available* to all people, is based in part upon the unity of God.[185] By denying that all can come to Christ in faith, meaning the universality of justification by faith, Calvinism also denies the universality of God, who created all in His image. This is a glaring theological weakness.

## 13. Hermeneutical Weakness

Calvinism is far too "mechanical" in its hermeneutic. Generally speaking, Calvinism does not take into consideration the various nuances of words and their uses. As a purview, it tends to eye all Scripture through the "grid" of election, thus leading to distortion. Moreover, sometimes Scripture teaches that the Father *gave* or *drew* people to Christ: the Father gives (John 6:37), the Father draws (John 6:44), the Father grants (John 6:65), and the Father has given (John 10:29). But, it is sometimes said that Christ and people *choose*: some of His own chose not to receive Him (John 1:11); some of His own people opted to receive Him (John 1:12); to receive stresses human responsibility and choice; some choose not to believe (John 3:18); some choose darkness over light (John 3:19); Jesus chose the twelve

---

[184] MacGorman, 45.
[185] J. P. McBeth, 125.

(John 6:70); some choose to keep Christ's sayings (John 12:47);[186] rejection implies choice (John 12:48); Jesus chooses and appoints that believers should bear fruit that remains (John 15:16); and, the individual calls upon Christ for salvation (Rom. 10:13). These textual citations belie the fact that Calvinism fails miserably to reconcile biblical paradoxes. The incarnation paradigm is one of the greatest hermeneutical tools ever given to us by God. It demands that seemingly contradictory statements be reconciled by positing a both/and solution rather than insisting on an either/or imbalance, as we saw in our review of Christological perspectives in another section. The both/and of hermeneutics is essential to accurate biblical interpretation. Those who fail to see this flunk at biblical exegesis. Calvinism has a hermeneutical weakness which it cannot overcome unless it jettisons Augustine's Neoplatonism, Calvin's either/or rigidity, and Matthew Henry's allegorizing, to name only a few pieces of hermeneutical baggage needing to be discarded. The best hermeneutical approach, and the one taught uncompromisingly by evangelical seminaries, is the grammatical-historical hermeneutic, which stresses components of its namesake, grammar and history, while also recognizing the presence of parable, allegory, paradox, parallelism, pericope, simile, poetry, and prose, just to name a few literary devices employed by the inspired writers of our infallible and inerrant Scriptures. Since monumental hermeneutical gymnastics are being done in order to keep Calvinism's tulip tenets afloat, as this present undertaking is demonstrating, it has a severe weakness which requires that its affinities with sixteenth century Scholasticism and its inability to maintain appropriate tension between the paradoxical both/ands of Scripture be thrown overboard in order that the exegetical ship not be overrun with sea water. Calvinism has a direful hermeneutical weakness.

---

[186] Alfred Plummer, *The Gospel According to St. John*, in *Thornapple Commentaries* (Cambridge, England: Cambridge University Press, 1882; reprint, Grand Rapids, MI: Baker Book House, 1981), 300.

## 14. Persuasive Weakness

The Bible urges people, even the "elect," not to stiffen their necks, but to yield to the Lord (2 Chron. 30:8). Paul reasoned in the synagogue of Corinth, seeking to *persuade* people to believe in Christ (Acts 18:4). Paul said that he *persuaded* men to worship God (Acts 18:13). Paul wrote that he reasoned and *persuaded* in the synagogue at Ephesus (Acts 19:8). Paul asserted that he sought to *persuade* people in Rome about Jesus (Acts 28:23). Some people are persuaded, while others simply will not believe, not *cannot* believe (Acts 28:24).

Knowing the fear and terror of the Lord establishes an urgency for *persuading* people to come to Christ now (2 Cor. 5:11). We see that Paul *begged* people to be reconciled to God (2 Cor. 5:20). He even warned that the grace of God could be received (heard) in vain (2 Cor. 6:1). He went on to say that now is the time for salvation (2 Cor. 6:2). So why persuade if grace is irresistible? What is the urgency if election is unconditional?

The use of persuasion necessitates choice, especially in the matter of salvation. Urgency implies that there is no time to waste in making the decision for Christ, since eternity is at stake. God's normative way is not coercion, but to draw, woo, and court. The Holy Spirit of God is received voluntarily, not involuntarily, as is evidenced by *labete*, the second aorist (which means past tense) active (voice), imperative of *lambano* found in John 20:22. If salvation only includes the divine element passively acting upon the person, as Calvinism claims, what is one to do with John 20:22? To be sure, Eph. 2:8-9 expresses the passivity of salvation when it asserts that by grace we have *been* saved through faith. But, once again, I appeal to the incarnation paradigm to help us grasp the both/and elements of the salvation event. Salvation requires both the divine element passively at work on man in the form of God's grace and the human element actively responding in faith. This is simply competent hermeneutics. Since persuasion is employed, man has a freewill and must actively respond to God's passive work. In so far as Calvinism does not adequately account for the clear testimony of Scripture as it relates to persuasion, Calvinism brandishes a grievous persuasive weakness.

## 15. Prayer Weakness

Before God punishes, He pleads (recall the preaching of Noah and the ministry of Jonah). This is not merely to ease His conscience. The very concept of prayer refutes both fatalism and determinism, since things need to be asked for, nothing is automatic, particularly salvation. Prayer is real and supplication is effective. Get this: prayer includes both the human and the divine elements. Think of the incarnation paradigm. We pray -- God responds. We express our needs, desires, and petitions and God answers yes, no, or wait awhile. Further, we seek to discern the mind of Christ so as not to pray selfishly (James 4:3). Now, since we can all go to God in prayer because He is fatherly toward everyone, in that all have been created in His image and He cares for us all, even more than He cares for a bird, prayer becomes practically meaningless for the true Calvinist, since, if he is consistent in his Calvinistic worldview, to him all things have been decided in advance. To the truly uniform Calvinist it would be absurd to pray for the salvation of the lost; it would only be appropriate to pray for the realized salvation of the elect. But even this revelatory event is timed already and cannot be altered, that is if the Calvinists are correct, which I argue they are not. Millions of Christians have seen the need for prayer and experienced its power. God wants people everywhere to pray to Him and Him alone. And our prayers make a difference, not because we "name and claim," but because God the Father wants what is best for us, yet refuses to force it upon us, choosing instead to wait patiently until we set our wills and our very selves before Him and long for His direction and prompting to have priority in our lives. Calvinism has a lamentable prayer weakness.

## 16. Historical Weakness

The fact that the doctrines attached to Calvinism were left largely undeveloped until about the time of Augustine makes it, as a system, highly suspicious. Aggressive evangelism coupled with 300 years of silence on the matter strongly suggest that Calvinism was not only unbelievable to the Apostles and their disciples, but was also relatively unknown to them as well. Then, Augustine's use of Neoplatonism in his hermeneutic, and his penchant to incorporate paganism into his theology (e.g., infant baptism) cast great suspicion on the doctrinal soundness of anything he wrote. Even reincarnationists boast that the ideas of Neoplatonism had a powerful effect upon the early Christian Church, or at least among the "elect few" of the early fathers of the Church.[187] Now, if reincarnationists are comfortable with Neoplatonism, and even recognize its effects on early church fathers, Christians should neither be at ease with its theological pronouncements nor ignorant of its prevalence with men like Augustine.

Moreover, Calvinism appears to be more of a polemical reaction to Pelagianism and works-based salvation than a genuine Bible doctrine. Therefore, the context of the time in which this doctrinal system emerged played a major part in its development. This historical weakness cannot be overlooked.

## 17. Petitioning Weakness

There is no biblical account of Jesus ever refusing to save, heal, or help anybody who asked. While there appear to be cases of reluctance regarding Gentiles which seem to be linked to God's timing for Jesus' messianic disclosure, Jesus always granted wholesome petitions - always. This fact further bolsters the inclusive nature of His mission. Moses declared that those who seek the Lord are guaranteed of finding Him (Deut. 4:29). Solomon stated that the priceless treasures of wisdom are for all (Prov. 8:4) and that those who seek the wisdom and knowledge of God find it (Prov. 8:17). God said, through Jeremiah, that those

---

[187] Atkinson, 108.

who seek Him, find Him (Jer. 29:13). Jesus told Nicodemus that those who *believe* will understand (John 3:21). By the way, notice here the importance of personal faith as the activator of understanding. Lastly, John recorded that Jesus stood in the midst of what was, doubtlessly, a large crowd, since this was uttered during the time of a feast, and cried out, shouting that any who thirst can come to Him and drink (John 7:37). Calvinism has an insurmountable petitioning weakness.

## 18. Simplistic Weakness

The doctrines of Calvinism are not arrived at by a simple reading of Scripture, but rather, mostly through outside influences. Just as Neoplatonism and deterministic Greek philosophy influenced Augustine more than the Bible influenced him, Calvinism lacks the basic, face-value simplicity rendered by grammatical-historical biblical interpretation. Allowing our ideas and worldview to be commanded by any person or thing other than God's self-revelation as disclosed in Scripture is to espouse an ideology instead of a theology. Ideologies are propped up by men whereas theology is undergirded by God through His Word. Calvinism has a simplistic weakness when it comes to arriving at its conclusions through an unassuming reading of Scripture apart from outside influences. The doctrines of total depravity, as the Calvinist understands it, unconditional election, limited atonement, and irresistible grace simply cannot be derived from a simple reading of Scripture. Other outside influences must be exerted in order for one to arrive at Calvinism's conclusions because the Bible does not lead anyone down these roads.

## 19. Citational Weakness

Comparatively speaking, Calvinism possesses only a handful of Scriptures to champion its opinion, and those are not balanced evenly with Scriptures which assert otherwise (remember the paradoxes which demand both/and interpretation). The number of these texts in comparison to passages which teach otherwise (listed and discussed throughout this manuscript) is quite disproportionate. A doctrine espousing total depravity, as Calvinism defines it, unconditional election, limited atonement, and irresistible grace is far too vast to be cited only a small number of times in the New Testament, which bleeds the theme of redemption on every page. Had God intended for man to embrace these four controversial points of Calvinism, He would have communicated them with greater frequency, citationally speaking, and through many biblical writers. But, this did not happen. Therefore, Calvinism encounters a painful citational weakness which cannot be denied.

## 20. Canonical Weakness

Those holding to Calvinism are generally guilty of developing a "canon within a canon." This means they have what amounts to a Bible within the Bible. They commonly employ an authoritative group of texts that are elevated to a level of supremacy. Frequently, they make use of a particular biblical writer who is referenced almost exclusively, usually Paul. Any teacher or teaching that does this is to be approached with extreme caution, particularly when the "canon" is primarily penned by one human agent. Most truly biblical doctrinal texts appear over and over in book after book, inspired from the breath of God through the pens of many biblical writers. Calvinism has a terrible canonical weakness, which should do more than raise eyebrows, it should spell danger with reference to the hermeneutical (interpretive) approach being employed.

## 21. Adamic Weakness

Just as Adam represents the failure of the entire human race, likewise does Jesus, the second Adam, represent the success in atoning for the failure of the entire human race (1 Cor. 15:21-22). However, this in no way implies Universalism, since the atoning work of Christ must be personally appropriated before it becomes efficacious. The unrighteousness of Adam affected all who are born. The righteousness of Jesus affects all who are born again. Adam's sinfulness tainted us. Jesus' sinlessness purifies us. Calvinism fails to correlate befittingly the *disease* of the entire human race in Adam with the *cure* for the entire human race in Jesus. Thus, Calvinism has an Adamic weakness in so far as it refuses to balance the scope of the remedy with the range of the plague.

## 22. Imbalance Weakness

As Universalism is out of balance to the left, Calvinism is out of balance to the right. Universalism is the false, and so-called Christian, teaching that all people are going to heaven. Notice the imbalance of both Calvinism and Universalism. Universalism is too inclusive; Calvinism is too exclusive. The truth is found in between. The incarnation paradigm is helpful here too, reminding us of the balance between the two natures of Jesus Christ, who was 100 percent divine and 100 percent human. Jesus Christ died for all but only those who appropriate His redemptive work by faith and repentance will be saved. Calvinism has a dreadful imbalance weakness.

## 23. Faith Weakness

Israel as a nation was elected but not all Israelites became believers. This raises questions about the theories of unconditional election and irresistible grace. This further raises questions as to how unbelief can be present among the elect. The Jews thought that, because they were related to Abraham, they did not need to repent and believe, but they were wrong, something which the Bible makes abundantly clear (Matt. 3:9). So then, faith was not produced in the elect or spawned by regeneration, as Calvinists teach. Faith is man's response to God's call and must precede regeneration. Calvinism has a conspicuous faith weakness.

## 24. Carnality Weakness

Calvinism fails miserably to account for carnal Christianity. The fact that there are carnal Christians (1 Cor. 3:1-4) begs the question as to why God made some carnal and some spiritual! Moreover, if there are carnal Christians, and there are, but carnality is not God's will for any Christian, then it is the believer himself or herself who must be accountable for the carnality, not God. Calvinism has a carnality weakness for which it cannot account.

## 25. Benevolent Weakness

Calvinism casts doubt on the benevolent character of God, portraying Him, rather, as malevolent, namely toward the non-elect. While it is an indubitable truth that the Bible speaks very clearly regarding the fact that all human beings are created with a sin nature (Rom. 3:23), it is equally true that the benevolent light of God refuses not to shine on every human heart. All human beings, in spite of being born with a wickedly sinful nature, begin life in the benevolent light of God, that is to say are objects of God's favor and in His redemptive "cross hairs" because of having been created in His image. It is unbelievers who will experience His wrath because of their refusal to turn in faith and repentance to Him. Calvinism has a benevolent weakness in that it minimizes, even neutralizes, the compassionate nature of the Creator toward the crown of His creative activity - humans.

# CONCLUSION

The doctrine known as five-point Calvinism is a classic example of truth out of balance. Characterized by bits of truth and seemingly supportive Scripture, then cleverly pieced together like a jig-saw puzzle, with more inference and eisegesis than fact and exegesis, it shares affinities with the Christological controversies of the Dark Ages and the Gnosticism encountered by believers of the first Christian centuries; and, as the article of W. R. Estep expresses, has not been warmly welcomed by the majority of evangelicals in general or by Southern Baptists in particular since the denomination began in 1845.[188] He reports that Baptists arose out of the English Puritan-Separatists movement, which *was* Calvinistic, but that these Baptists modified their Calvinism to a great degree. He further contends that the first English Baptists of record (ca. 1608) came to be known as "General Baptists," since they believed in a general, not a particular atonement, thus virtually denying the "L" in the "TULIP Theory," which, remember, stands for limited atonement. Estep says that other vestiges of their Calvinism almost completely vanished due to Anabaptist-Mennonite influence, and that even the Particular Baptists (ca. 1641), who believed in a limited, or particular, atonement also modified their Calvinism due to the influence of Menno Simons' writing entitled, *Foundation Book.* Estep affirms that, although there have been some Baptists who have embraced Calvinism over the years, the vast majority of Baptists "have never been doctrinaire Calvinists," as a careful study of the literary sources reveals. Walter Shurden, former Professor of Church History and Dean of The School of Theology at The Southern Baptist Theological Seminary, contends that the Anti-Missions Controversy (1820-1840) helped chart the theological course

---

[188] Estep, 12.

for future Southern Baptists, ruling out "hyper-Calvinism." He states that missionary-minded Baptists of the South continued to affirm the sovereignty of God in human history, but refused to emphasize this tenet when it undercut human responsibility. He concludes that, "Southern Baptists came out of the missionary melee believing that man is more than a puppet."[189]

Moreover, the basic position of 90 percent of Christianity and 96 percent of Southern Baptists is that Calvinism is false. I obtained the 90 percent figure straight from a leading Calvinistic scholar, R. C. Sproul, at a two-day seminar which I attended at Sagemont Church in Houston, Texas, in October 1998, where Sproul was the keynote speaker. He said that 90 percent of Christianity rejects Calvinism and its tenets. The 96 percent figure is a result of some research I did when I was serving as pastor of an Oklahoma church affiliated with the Tulsa Metro Baptist Association. At that time, along about 1998, there were approximately 142 Southern Baptist churches which participated in the Tulsa Metro Baptist Association. Of these, it was known that five were Calvinistic, and not all of them were openly Calvinistic. Dividing five by 142 suggests that roughly 96.5 percent of the churches rejected four or more of the five points of Calvinism. Although it cannot be concluded with certainty, these figures may be ballpark reflections of other Southern Baptists Associations as well. But recent trends suggest that Calvinism is on the rise among Southern Baptists.

H. Leon McBeth, former Professor of Church History at Southwestern Baptist Theological Seminary in Fort Worth, Texas, in his monumental work *The Baptist Heritage*, published in 1987, posits that, although no statistics existed, there were about four hundred Southern Baptist pastors who had some degree of allegiance to the new Calvinistic movement.[190] In light of the fact that there were approximately forty thousand Southern Baptist pastors when McBeth wrote his book, this means 1 percent or less were Calvinistic and approximately 99 percent

---

[189] Walter B. Shurden, *Not a Silent People* (Nashville, TN: Broadman Press, 1972), 47.

[190] H. Leon McBeth, *The Baptist Heritage* (Nashville, TN: Broadman Press, 1987), 774.

were not. McBeth also reports that the New Hampshire Confession of 1833 reflected Calvinism, and that the two Southern Baptist confessions of 1925 and 1963 retained some Calvinistic emphases, but "muted" and balanced them somewhat by heavy emphasis on evangelism, missions, and Christian responsibility.[191] This "modified Calvinism" is consistent with White's assessment of Southern Baptists beliefs, which he says retained both Arminian and Calvinistic elements, thus forming a distinctively unique system of thought.[192] Evidence of this is reflected in article six, "The Freeness of Salvation," of the 1925 *Baptist Faith and Message,* which states,

> The blessings of salvation are made free to all by the gospel. It is the duty of all to accept them by penitent and obedient faith. Nothing prevents the salvation of the greatest sinner except his own voluntary refusal to accept Jesus Christ as teacher, Saviour, and Lord.[193]

Under article seven, "Regeneration," the same confessional statement calls regeneration, "A work of God's free grace conditioned upon faith in Christ."[194] The words "conditioned upon faith" suggest the necessity of mankind's response and challenge the Calvinistic definition of total depravity, the claim of unconditional predestination, the tenet of irresistible grace, and the notion that regeneration precedes faith. Similarly, Herschel Hobbs argues that,

> Man is a person endowed with understanding and the privilege of choice. He is a person, not a puppet. God does not coerce man against his will. He is free to choose.[195]

All have sinned and fall short of perfection; but mankind's mind is not rendered so unreliable that he cannot comprehend the gospel and

---

[191] Ibid.
[192] White, 19.
[193] Ibid, 74-5.
[194] Ibid., 75.
[195] Hobbs, *Baptist Faith and Message,* 8.

respond affirmatively to God's grace. John R. W. Stott, Anglican New Testament scholar and author, echoes the dominant evangelical stance regarding total depravity when he writes, "It has never meant that every human being is as depraved as he could possibly be, but that every part of our humanness, including our mind, has become distorted by the Fall."[196] This is consistent with the words of Dale Moody, longtime Professor of New Testament at The Southern Baptist Theological Seminary in Louisville, Kentucky, in his exposition of *Romans*, in *The Broadman Bible Commentary*, where he argues that sin distorts but does not destroy the possibility of perception, pointing out that the mind may either become reprobate (Rom. 1:28) or be renewed (Rom. 12:2).[197] We have also seen this same stance taken in an earlier section by evangelical scholar John Newport.

There is no unconditional election. Mankind can say "no" to God. There is no such thing as an election which leaves the so-called "non-elect" to suffer eternal judgment with no hope of salvation. All humans can say "yes" to Christ. God's Holy Spirit provides grace for all. Additionally, the Bible plainly states that hell was prepared for the devil and his angels, not for people (Matt. 25:41). If anyone goes to hell it will literally be over the crucified and resurrected body of the Lord Jesus Christ. Unconditional election, as taught by Calvinism, would mean that those who are not elected, having no hope of salvation, are headed to hell, thus implying that hell was prepared for them too.

There is no such thing as a limited atonement. The work of Christ on the cross was for the sins of the world. Biblical support for this doctrine is completely missing or opined ignorantly.

The grace of God can be resisted. Read the Bible and see for yourself. Then just take a look around.

Since Israel was elected, yet some of the Israelites refused God and were subsequently rejected by Him, election never means automatic salvation. Some of the elect did not persevere because they said "no" to

---

[196] John R. W. Stott, *Decisive Issues Facing Christians Today* (Grand Rapids, MI: Fleming H. Revell Co., 1996), 32.

[197] Moody, 170.

God. Those who genuinely say "yes" to God are saved and cannot fall from salvation. There is security for the believer, but not an automatic salvation of the elect. The elect must also place personal faith in Christ.

Calvinism is long on disseminating information but short on elaborating upon the implications for life and theology that such a system of thought and interpretive methodology produces; and Calvinism is more than a theological framework, it is a worldview, eyeing everything through a distorted grid. Not only is Calvinism unbiblical, it is also unreasonable and it simply does not provide suitable answers to the complexities of life. Further, it is unimaginable to suppose that the Apostle Paul, having been redeemed out of Judaism from among the so-called elect, would retain such an erroneously exclusive understanding of election and predestination, and then disseminate it to the Gentile world. Paul did not believe God's redemptive plan was exclusive of anyone except those who refused to trust Christ. He firmly believed that God's salvific activity was broad enough to include all of humanity, although contingent upon the active response of each individual. Therefore, it is ludicrous to think that Paul preached anything but an inclusive gospel message, meaning that the gospel was for all people, on his missionary campaigns. Like the lesson of Peter's vision in Acts 10:9-16, Paul had also learned that, in God's eyes, every human being is worth redeeming. The mandate to evangelize Gentile and Jew encompasses all of humanity, which in effect describes the scope of God's redemptive intention: all those created in His image.

Finally, Calvinism seems to appeal primarily to idealists and intellectuals who are attracted to philosophical and theological systems of thought characterized by either/or absolutes. Thus, it is terribly inept at harmonizing Scripture that demands a both/and approach in order to ensure accurate interpretation, especially when it comes to understanding biblical paradoxes. Following the model of the incarnation paradigm, salvation presents Bible readers with a paradox. Such a paradox is even suggested in the command of Phil. 2:12 to work out our own salvation, which emphasizes the human element in, at the very least, the sanctification stage of redemption, and the declaration of Phil. 2:13 explaining that God is at work in every Christian, thus stressing the divine element in the sanctification stage of redemption. Salvation, then, is not a "let go and let God" matter but a "take hold with God" event.

The strengths of Calvinism notwithstanding, its weaknesses are far too glaring to overlook. Given its weaknesses, one is constrained to conclude with certainty that Calvinism is not a biblical doctrine to be perpetuated and faithfully guarded; but is, rather, an unsound teaching to be exposed and denounced. It is high time evangelical Christians liberate people from these invalid ideas, from the grip of narrowly conceived hermeneutics bent on producing a limited gospel and a restricted scope, and from the carnal passions and racial prejudices of the past. The Calvinistic definitions of "election" and "predestination" remind that when you marry a word, you may not want all the relatives. As Frank Page has written relative to Eph. 1:4-5, God "predestined the how, not the who."[198] We must passionately persuade others to worship Jesus Christ because the Bible teaches us to do so and because it also tells us that they can. And He cannot *be* worshiped unless he has created beings who are free. For if the triune God is to *be* worshiped (passive voice), man must be free, because if the worship of God by certain ones is determined by God, then their worship is not free, and if their worship is not free, then it is not that God is *being* worshiped, but rather that He is in effect worshiping Himself through human instrumentality, which is a disgusting theological proposition. Therefore, we are free to worship Him and we must passionately persuade others to worship Him too, for we are constrained by the transparently pure biblical axiom that it is not the will of our Father who is in heaven that even one little child perish, no not even one (Matt. 18:14).

---

[198] Frank S. Page, *Trouble with the Tulip: A Closer Examination of the Five Points of Calvinism*, 2d, ed. (Canton, GA: Riverstone Publishing Group, 2006), 60.

# APPENDIX A

The following information includes a brief biographical sketch of many of the sources cited in this manuscript at the time they wrote their works. Some of their writings did not include biographical sketches. Not all bibliographic entries are sketched.

Classification as a basic five-point Calvinist is indicated by an asterisk (\*) before the name. No asterisk indicates a non-five-point Calvinist as determined by reading the writings of each author. A question mark (?) indicates uncertainty on my behalf to determine the author's position.

Baker, Robert A. A.B., Baylor University; Th.M., Th.D., Southwestern Baptist Theological Seminary; Ph.D., Yale University; Professor of Church History, Southwestern Baptist Theological Seminary, Fort Worth, Texas.

Baxter, J. Sidlow.

\*Boettner, Loraine. B.S., Th.M., D.D., Litt.D. Theological writer.

Conner, W. T. Professor of Theology at Southwestern Baptist Theological Seminary from 1910-1949. He taught the doctrine of total depravity (I am unsure how he defined this), the doctrine of election from eternity of individuals to salvation, but not election to reprobation, and the doctrine of the perseverance of the saints. He never taught the doctrines of a limited atonement and an irresistible grace.[199]

---

[199] James Leo Garrett, Jr. "W. T. Conner: Contemporary Theologian," *Southwestern Journal of Theology* (Spring 1983): 43-60.

Estep, William R. GB.A., Berea College; Th.M., The Southern Baptist Theological Seminary; Th.D., Southwestern Baptist Theological Seminary; Distinguished Professor of Church History, Emeritus, Southwestern Baptist Theological Seminary, Fort Worth, Texas.

Finney, Charles G. Evangelist and Professor.

?Glass, Ron. Ph.D. Associate Professor of Bible Exposition, Talbot School of Theology, La Mirada, California.

Gonzales, Justo L. M.A., Ph.D., Yale University. Faculty Member, Interdenominational Theological Center, Atlanta, Georgia.

?Henry, Matthew. Presbyterian minister (1662-1714). In his commentary on Romans he appears to deny Calvinism's definition of total depravity when he writes, "Conscience is that candle of the Lord which was not quite put out, no, not in the Gentile world" (6:377). When speaking of justifying faith in this same commentary Henry writes, "It is to all, and upon all, those that believe. In this expression he inculcates that which he had been often harping upon, that Jews and Gentiles, if they believe, stand upon the same level, and alike are welcome to God through Christ; for there is no difference. Or, it is *eis pantas* - unto all, offered to all in general; the gospel excludes none that do not exclude themselves" (6:386). This suggests he, too, believed that Scripture taught the concept of a general atonement. Further, he writes, "Can it be imagined that a God of infinite love and mercy should limit and confine his favours to that little perverse people of the Jews, leaving all the rest of the children of men in a condition eternally desperate?" (6:388). Additionally, he states, "There is a free gift come upon all men, that is, it is made and offered promiscuously to all. The salvation wrought is a common salvation; the proposals are general, the tender free; whoever will may come, and take of these waters of life" (6:400). Then, he confusedly follows this statement by penning, "Many shall be made righteous - many compared with one, or as many as belong to the election of grace, which, though but a few as they are scattered up and down in the world, yet will be a great many when they come all together" (6:400)! Further, in his commentary on Jude he opines, "The gospel salvation is a common salvation, that is, in a most sincere offer and tender of it to all mankind to whom the notice of it reaches: for so the commission runs." He adds, "Surely God means as he speaks; he does not delude us with vain words, whatever men do; and therefore none are excluded from the benefit of these gracious offers and invitations, but those who obstinately, impenitently, finally exclude themselves" (6:1109).

Hobbs, Herschel H. D.D., Howard College; Th.M., Ph.D., The Southern Baptist Theological Seminary; longtime Southern Baptist pastor, writer, and denominational activist.

Humphreys, Fisher. B.A., Mississippi College; M.A., Loyola University; M.Litt., Oxford University; B.D., Th.D., New Orleans Baptist Theological Seminary. Professor of Divinity at the Beeson Divinity School of Samford University, Birmingham, Alabama, and former Professor of Theology at New Orleans Baptist Theological Seminary.

Hunt, Boyd. B.A., Wheaton College; Th.M., Th.D., Southwestern Baptist Theological Seminary; Distinguished Professor of Theology, Emeritus, Southwestern Baptist Theological Seminary, Fort Worth, Texas.

Lewis, C. S. Professor of Medieval and Renaissance Literature, Cambridge University.

MacGorman, J. W. B.A., University of Texas; M.Div., Th.D., Southwestern Baptist Theological Seminary; Ph.D., Duke University. Chairman of the New Testament Department at Southwestern Baptist Theological Seminary, Fort Worth, Texas.

McBeth, H. Leon. B.A., Wayland Baptist University; M.Div., Th.D., Southwestern Baptist Theological Seminary; Professor of Church History, Southwestern Baptist Theological Seminary, Fort Worth, Texas.

McGrath, Alister E. Ph.D., Oxford University; Lecturer in Christian Doctrine and Ethics, Wycliffe Hall, Oxford, England.

Mickelsen, A. Berkeley. B.D., Ph.D. Professor of Bible and Theology, Graduate School, Wheaton College, Wheaton, Illinois.

Moody, Dale. Professor of New Testament, The Southern Baptist Theological Seminary, Louisville, Kentucky.

Morgan, G. Campbell. Congregationalist Pastor of Westminster Chapel in London beginning in 1904. In his sermon "The Wages of Sin - The Gift of God" (*The Westminster Pulpit*, vol. 9) Morgan endorses the general atonement and effectively denies belief in a limited atonement by writing, "But if this soul who knows the gospel cannot escape from sin, it is equally true that it cannot escape from the gift which is placed at its disposal in the gospel. The gospel is the announcement of the fact that God has placed at the disposal of every soul the gift of eternal life" (9:341). He further writes, "I can choose sin if I will. Grace will appeal to me, woo me, warn me, but it will not compel me nor can it" (9:350). These statements mark a virtual denial of belief in the Calvinistic concepts of total depravity, unconditional election, irresistible grace, and limited atonement.

*Murray, John. A.M., Th.M. Professor of Systematic Theology, Westminster Theological Seminary, Philadelphia, Pennsylvania.

*Nettles, Thomas J. B.A., Mississippi College; M.Div., Ph.D. Southwestern Baptist Theological Seminary; Professor of Historical Theology, The Southern Baptist Theological Seminary, Louisville, Kentucky.

Newport, John P. B.A., D.Litt., William Jewel College; M.A., Texas Christian University; Th.M., Th.D., The Southern Baptist Theological Seminary; Ph.D., University of Edinburgh; Distinguished Professor of Philosophy of Religion, Emeritus, Southwestern Baptist Theological Seminary, Fort Worth, Texas (d. 2000).[200]

*Packer, J. I. Ph.D. Senior Tutor, Tyndale Hall, Bristol, England.

Pinnock, Clark H. Professor of Systematic Theology, McMaster Divinity College, Hamilton, Ontario.

Plummer, Alfred. Anglican. Master of University College, Durham (1874-1902).

Rainer, Thom S. President of LifeWay and former Dean of the Billy Graham School of Missions, Evangelism and Church Growth, The Southern Baptist Theological Seminary, Louisville, Kentucky.

Richardson, Kurt A. D.Theol. Assistant Professor of Historical Theology, Southeastern Baptist Theological Seminary, Wake Forest, North Carolina.

Scarborough, L. R. President of Southwestern Baptist Theological Seminary, Fort Worth, Texas, from 1914-1945.

---

[200] It is also worth noting that in a doctoral seminar, held in October 1998 by John P. Newport, I discussed with him the number of faculty members at Southwestern Baptist Theological Seminary holding allegiance to Calvinism. Although retired as the Vice President for Academic Affairs and Provost, Newport remained the Special Advisor to the President of the seminary, maintained his office on campus, and continued to teach philosophy of religion courses at the doctoral level. His response was that there were no faculty members at Southwestern of the Calvinistic persuasion. In fact, the only one he could recall in the past twenty or so years was Thomas Nettles, who eventually went to Mid-America Seminary (not a Southern Baptist seminary), and later to The Southern Baptist Theological Seminary. However, E. Earle Ellis, who occupies an emeritus position at Southwestern, does hold the Calvinistic position. Dr. Newport served as my Faculty Supervisor for my doctoral work at Southwestern.

Shurden, Walter B. Dean, School of Theology, and Professor of Church History, The Southern Baptist Theological Seminary, Louisville, Kentucky.

*Singer, Gregg C. Ph.D. Chairman, Department of History, Catawba College, Salisbury, North Carolina.

Stott, John R. W. Anglican New Testament scholar.

*Van Til, Cornelius. Th.M., Ph.D. Professor of Apologetics, Westminster Theological Seminary, Philadelphia, Pennsylvania.

Vincent, Marvin R. D.D. Baldwin Professor of Sacred Literature, Union Theological Seminary, New York, New York.

?Wallace, Ronald S. B.Sc., Ph.D. Minister, Lothian Road Church (Church of Scotland), Edinburgh, Scotland.

*Weber, Otto. Professor of Reformed Theology, University of Göttingen, Germany (d. 1966).

White, W. R. Th.D. Southwestern Baptist Theological Seminary. Occupied the Chair of Missions at Southwestern Baptist Theological Seminary from 1923-1927. Served as president of Hardin-Simmons University and Baylor University.

Wuest, Kenneth S. Instructor in Greek, Moody Bible Institute, Chicago, Illinois.

# APPENDIX B

| RACISM | HINDUISM | CALVINISM |
|--------|----------|-----------|
| Racial determinism | Social determinism | Spiritual determinism |
| Racial superiority | Social superiority | Spiritual superiority |
| Racial election | Social election | Spiritual election |
| Racial caste | Social caste | Spiritual caste |
| Racial bigotry | Social bigotry | Spiritual bigotry |
| Racial prejudice | Social prejudice | Spiritual prejudice |
| Racial exclusivity | Social exclusivity | Spiritual exclusivity |

# SCRIPTURE INDEX

114

Romans

# BIBLIOGRAPHY

Adams, Bob, and Sheri. "The Doctrine of Salvation: Mediated through the Incarnational Missionary." *Southwestern Journal of Theology* (Spring 1993): 18-21.

Allison, Dale, and Nancy E. "The Doctrine of Salvation: Mediated through the Incarnational Missionary." *Southwestern Journal of Theology* (Spring 1993): 22-5.

Anders, Max. *Colossians.* In *Holman New Testament Commentary*, ed. Max Anders. Vol. 8, *Galatians, Ephesians, Philippians, & Colossians.* Nashville, TN: Broadman & Holman Publishers, 1999.

Ashcraft, Morris. *Revelation.* In *The Broadman Bible Commentary*, ed. Clifton J. Allen. Vol. 12, *General Articles, Hebrews - Revelation.* Nashville, TN: Broadman Press, 1970.

Atkinson, William Walker. *Reincarnation and the Law of Karma: A Study of the Old-New World-Doctrine of Rebirth, and Spiritual Cause and Effect.* N.p.: Yogi Publication Society, 1908.

Baker, Robert A. *A Summary of Christian History.* Nashville, TN: Broadman Press, 1959.

_____. *The Baptist March in History.* Nashville, TN: Convention Press, 1958.

*Baptist Faith and Message, The.* Nashville, TN: The Southern Baptist Convention, 2000. Reprint 2003.

Barrett, C. K. *The Epistle to the Romans.* New York, NY: Harper & Row, Publishers, 1957.

Baxter, J. Sidlow. "The Epistle to the Romans." In *Explore the Book*. Vol. 6, *Acts to Revelation*. London, England: Marshall, Morgan, & Scott, 1952.

Bettenson, Henry, ed. *Documents of the Christian Church*. 2d ed. New York, NY: Oxford University Press, 1967.

Beidelman, T. O. *Colonial Evangelism*. Bloomington, IN: Indiana University Press, 1982.

Boa, Kenneth, and William Kruidenier. *Romans*. In *Holman New Testament Commentary*, ed. Max Anders. Vol. 6, *Romans*. Nashville, TN: Broadman & Holman Publishers, 2000.

Boettner, Loraine. "Foreknowledge." In *Baker's Dictionary of Theology*, ed. Everett F. Harrison, Geoffrey W. Bromiley, and Carl F. H. Henry, 225. Grand Rapids, MI: Baker Book House, 1960.

————. "Predestination." In *Baker's Dictionary of Theology*, ed. Everett F. Harrison, Geoffrey W. Bromiley, and Carl F. H. Henry, 415-7. Grand Rapids, MI: Baker Book House, 1960.

Brown, David. *The Epistle of Paul the Apostle to the Romans*. In *Commentary Critical and Explanatory on the Whole Bible*. 1871. Reprint, Oak Harbor, WA: Logos Research Systems, Inc., 1998, electronic version.

Bunn, John T. "The Covenant with Abraham." *Biblical Illustrator*, Fall 1987, 10-3.

Calvin, John. *Institutes of the Christian Religion*. 4th ed. Trans. Henry Beveridge. N.p.: 1581. Reprint, *The New American Standard Electronic Bible Library*, La Habra, CA: The Lockman Foundation, 1999.

Chadwick, Owen. *A History of Christianity*. Great Britain: George Weidenfeld & Nicolson Ltd., n.d. Reprint, New York, NY: St. Martin's Press, 1995.

_____. *The Reformation*. New York, NY: Penguin Books, 1981.

Collins, A. O. "The Pharisees." *Biblical Illustrator*, Winter 1982, 32-4.

Crawley, Winston. *Global Mission: A Story to Tell: An Interpretation of Southern Baptist Foreign Missions*. Nashville, TN: Broadman Press, 1985.

Culpepper, R. Alan. "Son of Man." *Biblical Illustrator*, Winter 1985, 19-21.

Dominy, Bert B. "Spirit, Church, and Mission: Theological Implications of Pentecost." *Southwestern Journal of Theology* (Spring 1993): 34-9.

Ellis, E. Earle. "God's Sovereign Grace in Salvation and the Nature of Man's Free Will." *Southwestern Journal of Theology* (Summer 2002): 28-43.

Ellison, H. L. *Jonah*. In *The Expositor's Bible Commentary*, ed. Frank E. Gaebelein. Vol. 7, *Daniel - Minor Prophets*. Grand Rapids, MI: Zondervan Publishing House, 1985.

Erickson, Millard J. "Lordship Theology: The Current Controversy." *Southwestern Journal of Theology* (Spring 1991): 5-15.

Estep, William R. "Doctrines Lead to 'Dunghill' Prof Warns." (Texas) *Baptist Standard*. 26 March 1997.

Fry, C. George, James R. King, Eugene R. Swanger, and Herbert C. Wolf. *Great Asian Religions*. Grand Rapids, MI: Baker Book House, 1984.

Garrett, James Leo, Jr. "W. T. Conner: Contemporary Theologian." *Southwestern Journal of Theology* (Spring 1983): 43-60.

Geisler, Norman L. *Christian Apologetics*. Grand Rapids, MI: Baker Book House, 1976. Reprint, 2002.

Glass, Ron. "Election in the Old Testament." In *The Holman Bible Handbook*, ed. David S. Dockery, 402. Nashville, TN: Holman Bible Publishers, 1992.

Gonzales, Justo L. *The Story of Christianity: The Reformation to the Present Day*. Vol. 2. San Francisco, CA: Harper & Row, Publishers, 1985.

Halley, Henry H. "Romans." In *Halley's Bible Handbook*, sp. ed., 480-7. N.p.: Halley's Bible Handbook, Inc., 1927. Reprint, Minneapolis, MN: Zondervan Publishing House, 1964.

Hansen, Collin. "Young, Restless, Reformed." *Christianity Today*, September 2006, 32.

Hemphill, Ken. *The Antioch Effect: 8 Characteristics of Highly Effective Churches*. Nashville, TN: Broadman & Holman Publishers, 1994.

_____. *Empowering Kingdom Growth: The Heartbeat of God.* Nashville, TN: Broadman & Holman Publishers, 2004.

Henry, Matthew. *An Exposition with Practical Observations of the Gospel According to St. John*. In *Matthew Henry's Commentary on the Whole Bible*. Vol. 5, *Matthew to John*. Reprint, McLean, VA: McDonald Publishing Company, n.d.

_____. *An Exposition with Practical Observations of the Epistle of St. Paul to the Romans*. In *Matthew Henry's Commentary on the Whole Bible*. Vol. 6, *Acts to Revelation*. Reprint, McLean, VA: MacDonald Publishing Company, n.d.

Hobbs, Herschel H. *The Baptist Faith and Message*. Nashville, TN: Convention Press, 1981.

_____. *1-2 Thessalonians*. In *The Broadman Bible Commentary*, ed. Clifton J. Allen. Vol. 11, *2 Corinthians - Philemon*. Nashville, TN: Broadman Press, 1970.

Holtrop, Philip C. *The Bolsec Controversy on Predestination, from 1551 to 1555*. Vol. 1, Book 1. Lewiston, NY: The Edwin Mellen Press, 1993.

Hughes, Philip. *A Popular History of the Catholic Church*. Garden City, NY: Image Books, 1955.

Humphreys, Fisher, and Paul E. Robertson. *God So Loved the World: Traditional Baptists and Calvinism*. New Orleans, LA: Insight Press, 2000.

Hunt, Boyd. "The Person and Work of the Holy Spirit: The Effecter of God's Purpose." Seminary Hill Station, Fort Worth, TX: by the author, 1989.

_____. *Redeemed! Eschatological Redemption and the Kingdom of God*. Nashville, TN: Broadman & Holman Publishers, 1993.

Hunt, Dave. *What Love Is This? Calvinism's Misrepresentation of God*. Sisters, OR: Loyal Publishing, Inc., 2002.

Johnson, George, Jerome D. Hannan, and Sister M. Dominica. *The Story of the Church: Her Founding, Mission and Progress*. New York, NY: Benzinger Brothers, Inc., 1946.

Keil, C. F., and F. Delitzsch. *Biblical Commentary on the Old Testament. Jeremiah*, by C. F. Keil, vol. 8. Trans. James Kennedy. Reprint, Grand Rapids, MI: William B. Eerdmans Publishing Co., 1986.

Latourette, Kenneth Scott. *A History of the Expansion of Christianity: The Great Century: Europe and the United States: 1800-1914*. Vol. 4. New York, NY: Harper & Row, Publishers, 1941. Reprint, Grand Rapids, MI: Zondervan Publishing House, 1974.

_____. *Christianity in a Revolutionary Age: A History of Christianity in the 19th and 20th Centuries*. Vol. 2. New York, NY: Harper & Row, Publishers, 1959. Reprint, Grand Rapids, MI: Zondervan Publishing House, 1976.

Lewis, C. S. *Christian Reflections*. Grand Rapids, MI: William B. Eerdmans Publishing Co., 1967.

Luther, Martin. *The Bondage of the Will*. Trans. J. I. Packer and O. R. Johnston. N.p.: James Clarke & Co. Ltd., 1957. Reprint, Grand Rapids, MI: Fleming H. Revell, 2004.

MacGorman, John William. *Romans*. In *Layman's Bible Book Commentary*. Vol. 20, *Romans - 1 Corinthians*. Nashville, TN: Broadman Press, 1980.

Marsden, George M. *Fundamentalism and American Culture: The Shaping of Twentieth-Century Evangelicalism: 1870-1925*. New York, NY: Oxford University Press, 1982.

Marshall, Molly Truman. "The Doctrine of Salvation: Biblical-Theological Dimensions." *Southwestern Journal of Theology* (Spring 1993): 12-7.

Martin, Michael. "Fallen from Grace." *Biblical Illustrator*, Fall 1987, 37-9.

McBeth, H. Leon. *The Baptist Heritage: Four Centuries of Baptist Witness*. Nashville, TN: Broadman Press, 1987.

McBeth, J. P. *Exegetical and Practical Commentary on the Epistle to the Romans*. Dallas, TX: by the author, 1937.

McDowell, Edward A. *1-2-3 John*. In *The Broadman Bible Commentary*, ed. Clifton J. Allen. Vol. 12, *General Articles, Hebrews -Revelation*. Nashville, TN: Broadman Press, 1970.

McGrath, Alister E. *Justification by Faith: What It Means to Us Today*. Grand Rapids, MI: Academie Books, 1988.

_____. *The Mystery of the Cross*. Grand Rapids, MI: Academie Books by Zondervan Publishing House, 1988.

_____. *Understanding the Trinity*. Grand Rapids, MI: Academie Books by Zondervan Publishing House, 1988.

_____. *Evangelicalism & the Future of Christianity*. Downers Grove, IL: InterVarsity Press, 1995.

Mead, Frank S. *Handbook of Denominations in the United States*. 8th ed. Rev. Samuel S. Hill. Nashville, TN: Abingdon Press, 1985.

Mickelsen, A. Berkeley. *The Epistle to the Romans*. In *The Wycliffe Bible Commentary*, ed. Charles F. Pfeiffer and Everett F. Harrison. Nashville, TN: The Southwestern Company, 1962.

Mims, Gene. "Predestination." *Biblical Illustrator*, Fall 2003, 50-3.

Moody, Dale. *Romans*. In *The Broadman Bible Commentary*, ed. Clifton J. Allen. Vol. 10, *Acts - 1 Corinthians*. Nashville, TN: Broadman Press, 1970.

Morgan, G. Campbell. "Amazing Love." In *The Westminster Pulpit*. Vol. 1, 125-38. London, England: Hodder and Stoughton, 1906. Reprint, Grand Rapids, MI: Baker Book House, 1954.

_____. "Hope." In *The Westminster Pulpit*. Vol. 8, 75-86. London, England: Hodder and Stoughton, 1906. Reprint, Grand Rapids, MI: Baker Book House, 1954.

_____. "Horizoned by Resurrection." In *The Westminster Pulpit*. Vol. 4, 123-35. London, England: Hodder and Stoughton, 1906. Reprint, Grand Rapids, MI: Baker Book House, 1954.

_____. "Life; In Flesh, or in Spirit." In *The Westminster Pulpit*. Vol. 4, 97-109. London, England: Hodder and Stoughton, 1906. Reprint, Grand Rapids, MI: Baker Book House, 1954.

_____. "Promise at the Cross." In *The Westminster Pulpit*. Vol. 6, 113-26. London, England: Hodder and Stoughton, 1906. Reprint, Grand Rapids, MI: Baker Book House, 1954.

_____. "The Church's Debt to the World." In *The Westminster Pulpit*. Vol. 10, 226-37. London, England: Hodder and Stoughton, 1906. Reprint, Grand Rapids, MI: Baker Book House, 1954.

_____. "The First-Born." In *The Westminster Pulpit*. Vol. 8, 337-49. London, England: Hodder and Stoughton, 1906. Reprint, Grand Rapids, MI: Baker Book House, 1954.

_____. "The Justification of the Sinner." In *The Westminster Pulpit*. Vol. 9, 189-202. London, England: Hodder and Stoughton, 1906. Reprint, Grand Rapids, MI: Baker Book House, 1954.

_____. "The Power of the Gospel." In *The Westminster Pulpit*. Vol. 8, 284-96. London, England: Hodder and Stoughton, 1906. Reprint, Grand Rapids, MI: Baker Book House, 1954.

_____. "The Spirit of Christ; The Supreme Test." In *The Westminster Pulpit*. Vol. 4, 110-22. London, England: Hodder and Stoughton, 1906. Reprint, Grand Rapids, MI: Baker Book House, 1954.

_____. "The Spirit of Life." In *The Westminster Pulpit*. Vol. 1, 180-9. London, England: Hodder and Stoughton, 1906. Reprint, Grand Rapids, MI: Baker Book House, 1954.

_____. "The Wages of Sin - The Gift of God." In *The Westminster Pulpit*. Vol. 9, 340-51. London, England: Hodder and Stoughton, 1906. Reprint, Grand Rapids, MI: Baker Book House, 1954.

Murray, Iain H. *Spurgeon v. Hyper-Calvinism: The Battle for Gospel Preaching*. Carlisle, PA: The Banner of Truth Trust, 1995. Reprint, 2000.

Murray, John. "Elect, Election." In *Baker's Dictionary of Theology*, ed. Everett F. Harrison, Geoffrey W. Bromiley, and Carl F. H. Henry, 179-80. Grand Rapids, MI: Baker Book House, 1960.

Myers, Edward D., ed. *Christianity and Reason*. New York, NY: Oxford University Press, 1951.

Nettles, Thomas J. "L. R. Scarborough: Public Figure." *Southwestern Journal of Theology* (Spring 1983): 24-42.

_____. "Article 5a: God's Purpose of Grace and Election." *The Baptist Banner*, May 2004, 4.

Newport, John P. *The New Age Movement and the Biblical Worldview: Conflict and Dialogue.* Grand Rapids, MI: William B. Eerdmans Publishing Co., 1998.

_____. *What Is Christian Doctrine?* Nashville, TN: Broadman Press, 1984.

Norris, Richard A., Jr., ed. *The Christological Controversy.* Philadelphia, PA: Fortress Press, 1988.

Olson, C. Gordon. *Getting the Gospel Right: A Balanced View of Salvation Truth.* Cedar Knolls, NJ: Global Gospel Publishers, 2005.

Packer, J. I. "Election." In *The New Bible Dictionary*, ed. J. D. Douglas, 357-61. Grand Rapids, MI: William B. Eerdmans Publishing Co., 1962.

_____. "Predestination." In *The New Bible Dictionary*, ed. J. D. Douglas, 1024-6. Grand Rapids, MI: William B. Eerdmans Publishing Co., 1962.

_____. "Providence." In *The New Bible Dictionary*, ed. J. D. Douglas, 1050-2. Grand Rapids, MI: William B. Eerdmans Publishing Co., 1962.

Page, Frank S. *Trouble with the Tulip: A Closer Examination of the Five Points of Calvinism.* 2d ed. Canton, GA: Riverstone Group Publishing, 2006.

Parkhurst, Louis Gifford, Jr., *Principles of Liberty: More Great Themes on Romans from the Writings of Charles G. Finney.* Minneapolis, MN: Bethany House Publishers, 1983.

Pinnock, Clark H. *The Scripture Principle.* San Francisco, CA: Harper & Row, Publishers, 1984.

Plummer, Alfred. *The Gospel According to St. John.* In *Thornapple Commentaries.* Cambridge, England: Cambridge University Press, 1882. Reprint, Grand Rapids, MI: Baker Book House, 1981.

Polhill, John B. "No Respecter of Persons: God's View of Race Relations." *Biblical Illustrator,* Summer 1986, 66-71.

Powicke, Sir Maurice. *The Reformation in England.* New York, NY: Oxford University Press, 1967.

Rakestraw, Robert V. "The Persistent Vegetative State and the Withdrawal of Nutrition and Hydration." In *Readings in Christian Ethics.* Vol. 2. ed. David K. Clark and Robert V. Rakestraw. Grand Rapids, MI: Baker Book House, 1996.

Rainer, Thom S. *The Book of Church Growth: History, Theology, and Principles.* Nashville, TN: Broadman & Holman Publishers, 1993.

Richardson, Kurt A. "Election in the New Testament." In *The Holman Bible Handbook,* ed. David S. Dockery, 712. Nashville, TN: Holman Bible Publishers, 1992.

Robertson, Archibald Thomas. *The Epistle to the Romans.* In *Word Pictures in the New Testament.* Vol. 4, *Epistles of Paul.* Nashville, TN: The Sunday School Board of the Southern Baptist Convention, 1931. Reprint, Grand Rapids, MI: Baker Book House, n.d.

Routh, E. C. *Baptists on the March: A History of Baptists.* Shawnee, OK: Oklahoma Baptist University Press, n.d.

Saint Augustine. *Confessions.* Trans. Henry Chadwick. New York, NY: Oxford University Press, 1991. Reprint, 1998.

Shurden, Walter B. *Not a Silent People.* Nashville, TN: Broadman Press, 1972.

Singer, Gregg C. "Augustinianism." In *Baker's Dictionary of Theology*, ed. Everett F. Harrison, Geoffrey W. Bromiley, and Carl F. H. Henry, 80. Grand Rapids, MI: Baker Book House, 1960.

Smith, Henry N. "Salvation in the Face of Many Faiths: Toward a Hermeneutic of Optimism." *Southwestern Journal of Theology* (Spring 1993): 26-31.

Smith, William. "Epistle to the Romans." In *Smith's Bible Dictionary*, ed. F. N. and M. A. Peloubet, 568. N.p.: Porter and Coates, 1884. Reprint, Grand Rapids, MI: Zondervan Publishing House, 1981.

Stott, John R. W. *Decisive Issues Facing Christians Today*. Grand Rapids, MI: Fleming H. Revell Co., 1996.

Trammell, Timothy. "When John and Jesus Started Ministry." *Biblical Illustrator*, Winter 2000-01, 58-63.

Valentine, Foy. "The Contemporary Racial Crisis: A Christian Perspective." *Southwestern Journal of Theology* (April 1965): 17-29.

Van Til, Cornelius. "Calvinism." In *Baker's Dictionary of Theology*, ed. Everett F. Harrison, Geoffrey W. Bromiley, and Carl F. H. Henry, 109. Grand Rapids, MI: Baker Book House, 1960.

Vedder, Henry C. *A Short History of the Baptists*. N.p.: The American Baptist Publication Society, 1907. Reprint, Valley Forge, PA: Judson Press, 1978.

Vidler, Alec R. *The Church in an Age of Revolution*. New York, NY: Penguin Books, 1981.

Vincent, Marvin R. *The Epistle to the Romans*. In *Word Studies in the New Testament*. Vol. 3, *The Epistles of Paul*. New York, NY: Charles Scribner's Sons, 1887. Reprint, Grand Rapids, MI: William B. Eerdmans Publishing Co., 1980.

Wallace, Ronald S. "Christology." In *Baker's Dictionary of Theology*, ed. Everett F. Harrison, Geoffrey W. Bromiley, and Carl F. H. Henry, 117-23. Grand Rapids, MI: Baker Book House, 1960.

Walls, Jerry L., and Joseph R. Dongell. *Why I Am Not a Calvinist*. Downers Grove, IL: InterVarsity Press, 2004.

Weber, Otto. *Foundations of Dogmatics*. Vol. 1. Trans. Darrell L. Guder. Neukirchen, Germany.: Kreis Moers, 1955. Reprint, Grand Rapids, MI: William B. Eerdmans Publishing Co., 1988.

White, W. R. *Baptist Distinctives*. Nashville, TN: Convention Press, 1946.

Wuest, Kenneth S. *Romans*. In *Wuest's Word Studies*. Vol. 1, *Mark - Romans - Galatians - Ephesians and Colossians*. Grand Rapids, MI: William B. Eerdmans Publishing Co., 1955. Reprint, 1973.

_____. *2 Peter*. In *Wuest's Word Studies*. Vol. 2, *Philippians - Hebrews, The Pastoral Epistles, First Peter - Jude*. Grand Rapids, MI: William B. Eerdmans Publishing Co., 1954. Reprint, 1973.

Yarbrough, Slayden A. "Early Christianity's Exclusivism." *Biblical Illustrator*, Winter 1987, 15-8.

Young, Doyle L. "The Doctrine of Salvation: Baptist Views." *Southwestern Journal of Theology* (Spring 1993): 4-11.